The Poet and the Professor

6-8

Poems for Building Reading Skills

STAIRWAY TO THE STARS

They surround the Earth, five separate layers,
like giant atmospheric stairs,
which from our little earthly base
become our stairway into space.

The bottom layer is way down here;
we're walking in the *troposphere*.

Where airplanes fly it's cold and clear;
they're up there in the *stratosphere*.

Radio waves range far or near
bouncing off the *mesosphere*.

every season of the year,
the *thermosphere*.

tellites on the space-frontier
d and 'round in the *exosphere*.

he earth in separate layers,
mospheric stairs,
all alone,
known

EXOSPHERE
THERMOSPHERE
MESOSPHERE
STRATOSPHERE
TROPOSPHERE

Authors

Brod Bagert and Timothy Rasinski

Contributing Author

Kathleen Knoblock

SHELL EDUCATION

Publishing Credits

Dona Herweck Rice, *Editor-in-Chief*; Lee Aucoin, *Creative Director*; Don Tran, *Print Production Manager*; Timothy J. Bradley, *Illustration Manager*; Conni Medina, M.S.Ed., *Editorial Director*; Tamara Hollingsworth, *Editor*; Jodene Lynn Smith, M.A., *Editor*; Evelyn Garcia, *Associate Editor*; Robin Erickson, *Interior Layout Designer* ; Blanca Apodaca, Kelly Brownlee and Scott Valenzuela, *Illustrators*; Corinne Burton, *M.S.Ed., Publisher*

Prose and Poems © Brod Bagert 2010

McREL Standards © 2004 www.mcrel.org/standards-benchmarks

All recordings performed by Brod Bagert. Recorded, edited, and mastered by Ross Ricks at Surf City Sound. www. surfcitysound.com

Shell Education
5301 Oceanus Drive
Huntington Beach, CA 92649-1030
http://www.shelleducation.com
ISBN 978-0-7439-0240-0
©2010 Shell Educational Publishing, Inc.

Table of Contents

Developing students' reading skills is a critical goal that begins in the primary grades. Yet with each successive grade, students must acquire increasing skills at reading and understanding a variety of texts. *The Poet and the Professor: Poems for Building Reading Skills* provides valuable instructional tools and engaging materials and activities for increasing student skills in reading, writing, listening, and speaking. As you use the poems, lessons, and activities in this book, you will know that you are not only providing instruction based on solid educational research, but also giving students opportunities to learn and practice specific academic standards.

The Poet and the Professor: Poems for Building Reading Skills has been designed to provide high-interest instructional texts and lessons based on best practices in reading education. The concept of the book was developed by Dr. Timothy Rasinski, Professor of Literacy Education at Kent State University and author of numerous articles, books, and publications on reading education. The poems in this book were written by Brod Bagert, whose catchy and humorous books of poetry have entertained and inspired scores of young people to embrace poetry.

In its *Report of the National Reading Panel: Teaching Children to Read* (2006), the National Reading Panel noted predominant themes in the research on the development of reading comprehension skills. The core of *The Poet and the Professor: Poems for Building Reading Skills* revolves around the NRP's findings, specifically, 1) "Reading comprehension is a complex cognitive process that cannot be understood without a clear description of the role that vocabulary development and vocabulary instruction play in the understanding of what has been read,"

and 2) "Comprehension is an active process that requires an intentional and thoughtful interaction between the reader and the text."

Making Connections

Studies show that making connections—drawing upon prior knowledge, emotions, opinions, understandings, and experiences—helps students better understand what they are reading (Harvey and Goudvis 2000). Keene and Zimmermann (1997) concluded that students comprehend better when they make different kinds of connections: text-to-self, text-to-text, and text-to-world.

Text-to-self connections are those that are individual and personal. For example, in Lesson 26 of this book, prior to reading a poem about a girl with a unique style, students are asked to reflect on a time when someone made a negative comment about their appearance and how it made them feel.

Text-to-text connections are those that identify similarities between one thing that has been read (whether a whole book or a single word) and a new text. In other words, students use the familiar to help them understand the unfamiliar.

Text-to-world connections are those that are more global than personal. These include information or impressions students have acquired from such things as reading stories and watching movies (narrative); studying science or social studies (expository); seeing ads on TV or in magazines (persuasive); and participating in discussions. One goal of this book is to challenge students to draw upon their prior knowledge and experiences to prepare them to better understand what they will read.

Comprehension Strategies

Comprehension is defined as "intentional thinking during which meaning is constructed through interactions between text and reader" (Harris and Hodges 1995). In its findings, the National Reading Panel (2006) states that "the rationale for the explicit teaching of comprehension skills is that comprehension can be improved by teaching students to use specific cognitive strategies or to reason strategically when they encounter barriers to understanding what they are reading." The Panel further notes that "explicit or formal instruction in the application of comprehension strategies has been shown to be highly effective in enhancing understanding."

Effective reading instruction, then, must include teaching students strategies that they can employ as they read in order to increase comprehension. Hosenfeld (1993) states that expert readers freely and appropriately use a variety of strategies to gain understanding as they read. There are many effective strategies, including predicting, rephrasing, asking and answering questions (Bottomley and Osborn 1993) and using graphic organizers (Jensen 1998). Teaching and modeling reading comprehension strategies through structured and explicit instruction will enable students to learn how to comprehend text (Rosenshine and Meister 1994). The result of both explicit teaching and modeling is that students are learning when and how to use these strategies to construct meaning (Carter 1997).

Within the lessons of *The Poet and the Professor: Poems for Building Reading Skills*, numerous comprehension strategies are presented and explained, and students are given opportunities to apply these strategies. Each lesson focuses on a single strategy, but all lessons are in whole-group format, so students may learn from one another as well as from the teacher.

The goal of teaching a variety of comprehension strategies is to give students a cache of tools to call upon when interacting with any text. As students move from reading words to reading ideas, concepts, and information, they learn to use these tools more and more effectively. In essence, comprehension tools enable students to not just read what someone wrote but also to read what someone communicated.

Standards-Based Skills

In many states, teachers are required to demonstrate how their lessons meet state standards. Standards are statements that describe the knowledge, skills, and content students should acquire at each level. Standards are also used to develop standardized tests to evaluate students' academic progress.

Each lesson in *The Poet and the Professor: Poems for Building Reading Skills* is correlated to language arts standards for grades 6–8. See the correlation chart on pages 13–14 for the skills covered in this book.

Each Standards-Based Skill Focus section of the teacher page highlights a specific benchmark skill needed to achieve the overall standard. As you teach the standards-based skills in this book, you can be assured that they have been identified as appropriate for students in grades 6–8.

Vocabulary Word Study

The National Reading Panel (2006) recognizes the importance of vocabulary knowledge in the development of reading skills. After examining over 20,000 research citations, the panel concluded that studies suggest that "vocabulary instruction does lead to gains in comprehension," and that "vocabulary should be taught both directly and indirectly." The panel specifically mentions that "repetition and multiple exposures to vocabulary items are important" and that "learning in rich contexts enhances the acquisition of vocabulary."

Word knowledge and reading comprehension go hand in hand. In fact, "vocabulary knowledge is one of the best predictors of reading achievement" (Richek 2005). Further, "vocabulary knowledge promotes reading fluency, boosts reading comprehension, improves academic achievement, and enhances thinking and communication" (Bromley 2004). Noted reading scholar and researcher Michael Pressley (2001) states that vocabulary instruction has direct effects on reading comprehension. Students who understand the words they read are more likely to comprehend what they have read.

The Poet and the Professor: Poems for Building Reading Skills reflects the practices found to be effective by many researchers. These include:

- teaching vocabulary in a word-rich context
- teaching selected words intentionally while encouraging unintentional acquisition as well
- providing multiple types of information about words
- guiding students to make connections between known and unknown words
- using strategies that increase students' ability to learn new words on their own

For example, one strategy for learning new words is to use the context, as seen in the Vocabulary Word Study Section of Lesson 19. After locating targeted vocabulary words in the poem, students use the context of the poem to determine which of three related definitions apply. In the lesson, one of the targeted vocabulary words is *change*. Students must use the context of the sentence to determine if the word means: "coins", "to make different", or "to give or get smaller amounts of money."

Differentiation

Classrooms have evolved into diverse pools of learners with gifted students, English language learners, high achievers, learning-disabled students, underachievers, and average achievers. Teachers are expected to meet their diverse needs in one classroom. Differentiation encompasses what is taught, how it is taught, and the products students create to show what they have learned. These categories are often referred to as content, process, and product:

- Differentiating by content means putting more depth into the curriculum by organizing the curriculum concepts and structure of knowledge.
- Differentiating by process requires the use of varied instructional techniques and materials to enhance learning.
- Differentiating by product means that children are asked to show their learning in ways that will enhance their cognitive development and personal expression.

Teachers can keep these categories in mind as they plan instruction that will best meet the needs of their students.

Differentiating for Below-Grade-Level Students

Below-grade-level students will probably need concepts to be made more concrete for them. They may also need extra guidance in developing oral and written language. By receiving extra support and understanding, these students will feel more secure and have greater success. Suggested ideas include:

- Allow partner work for instructional activities.
- Allocate extra practice time.
- Allow for kinesthetic (hands-on) activities where appropriate.

Differentiating for Above-Grade-Level Students

These students usually learn concepts very quickly. The activities and end products can be adapted to be appropriate for individual students. Suggested ideas include:

- Assign students the activities that represent more complex concepts.
- Assign more complex oral and written responses.
- Have students design their own learning strategies and share them with the class.

Differentiating for English Language Learners

English language learners make up an ever-increasing percentage of our school-age population. Like all students, English language learners need teachers who have a strong knowledge base and commitment to developing students' language. It is crucial that teachers work carefully to develop English language learners' academic vocabularies. Teachers should keep in mind the following important practices:

- Create a comfortable atmosphere that encourages students to use language.
- Respect and draw on students' backgrounds and experiences and build connections between the known and the new.
- Model and scaffold language use.
- Make use of realia, concrete materials, visuals, pantomime, and other nonlinguistic representations of concepts to make input comprehensible. Write new words on the board as they are shared or provide each student with a set of cards that contain the words.
- Provide wait time to allow students time to put their thoughts into words.

Differentiating by Proficiency Levels for English Language Learners

All teachers should know the levels of language acquisition for each of their English language learners (ELLs). Knowing these levels will help to plan instruction. (The category titles vary from district to district or state to state, but the general descriptions are common.) Students at level 1 will need a lot of language support in all the activities. Using visuals to support oral and written language will help to make the language more comprehensible. These students "often understand much more than they are able to express" (Herrell and Jordan 2004). It is the teacher's job to move them from listening to language to expressing language. Students at levels 2 and 3 will benefit from pair work in speaking tasks, but they will need additional individual support during writing and reading tasks. Students at levels 4 and 5 (or 6, in some cases) may appear to be fully proficient in the English language. However, because they are English language learners, they may still struggle with comprehending the academic language used during instruction. They may also struggle with reading and writing.

The following chart shows the proficiency levels at a quick glance. The levels are based on the World-Class Instructional Design and Assessment (WIDA) Consortium (WIDA 2007).

Proficiency Levels at a Quick Glance

Proficiency Level	Questions to Ask	Activities/Actions		
Level 1—Entering minimal comprehension no verbal production	Where is…? What examples do you see? What are the parts of…?	listen	draw	mime
		point	circle	respond (one or two words)
Level 2—Beginning limited comprehension short spoken phrases	Can you list three…? What facts or ideas show…? What do the facts mean?	move	select	act/act out
		match	choose	list
Level 3—Developing increased comprehension simple sentences	How did ____ happen? Why do you think…? If you could __, what would you do?	name	list	respond (phrases or sentences)
		label	categorize	tell/say
Level 4—Expanding very good comprehension some errors in speech	How would you show…? What would result if…? Why is this important?	recall	retell	define
		compare/contrast	explain	summarize
		describe	role-play	restate
Level 5—Bridging comprehension comparable to native-English speakers speaks using complex sentences	What is meant by…? What is an original way to show…? Why is it better that…?	analyze	defend	complete
		evaluate	justify	support
		create	describe	express

How to Use This Book

The Poet and the Professor: Poems for Building Reading Skills is a succession of lessons built around a compilation of poems. The components are this book (which is a teacher's resource for using the poems to build reading skills), the Audio CD, and the Teacher Resource CD.

This book features original poems. Accompanying each poem is a lesson plan that contains the sections Making Connections, Comprehension Strategy, Standards-Based Skill Focus, and Vocabulary Word Study. Information and ideas about how to relate the poem to each of these areas is provided on this page. For more information about each section, see the Research section of the book (pp. 4–6). In addition, two activity pages are provided that relate to the Standards-Based Skill Focus and the Vocabulary Word Study sections of the lesson plan.

The Audio CD contains recordings of the prose and poems in the book. Students can follow the text on their own copies of the poem pages, on an interactive whiteboard, or on an overhead projector.

The Teacher Resource CD contains a variety of resources that can be used to enhance the lessons provided in this book. The poem pages can be photocopied on a transparency, displayed on an interactive whiteboard, or printed and copied for each student. The activity pages are included on the Teacher Resource CD. Finally, provided on the CD is a page-turning ebook that includes all of the poems used in this book. This page-turning ebook allows students to refer to all the poems in a digital format. This page-turning ebook can also be displayed on an interactive whiteboard for easy viewing during a whole-class lesson.

The Poet and the Professor: Poems for Building Reading Skills has been designed to supplement your regular reading language arts program. The following is a suggested routine for incorporating the poetry, reading comprehension, skills, and word study activities into your weekly lessons.

Day	Suggested Instructional Plan
Day 1	Before sharing the poem with students, prepare them for reading with the suggested discussion and activities in the Making Connections section of the lesson. Conclude by modeling fluent reading of the poem.
Day 2	Display the poem and/or provide a copy of the poem for each student. Begin by rereading the poem, modeling proper tone, expression, and pace. Encourage students to follow along as you read. Next, use the suggestions in the Comprehension Strategy section for whole-group teaching and discussion. Allow students to refer to the poem as they explore the strategies for understanding its literal and interpretive meaning. Day 2 would also be a good time to reread the poem several times, incorporating various fluency-building techniques. Suggested techniques include the following: • read-and-repeat (also known as echo reading, refrain reading, or call and response) • paired reading • choral reading (in a whole group or small groups, or as line-a-child) • reader's theater (performance reading) For detailed information about these techniques and more, see Rasinski (2003) in the References Cited section on page 143 of this book.
Day 3	Use Day 3 to concentrate on skill development. Begin with the suggested activities in the Standards-Based Skill Focus section of the lesson. Then give students the opportunity to apply the skill by completing the reproducible activity sheet that corresponds with the lesson.

Day	Suggested Instructional Plan
Day 4	Focus on vocabulary and word study. Begin with the activities suggested in the Vocabulary Word Study section of the lesson. Then reinforce the words and concepts introduced by having students complete the corresponding reproducible activity sheet. At the end of each Word Study page is an optional extension activity. You may use this as homework, extra credit, or a regular writing assignment to be done in class the following day.
Day 5	Choose one or more of the following suggested activities to wrap up the week's lesson: • Have students complete the extension activity from the Word Study page. • Take a few minutes of class time to review together the skill and word study pages students completed in this week's lesson. • Allow students to practice and then perform the poem for one another, you, or another class. • Have students keep a journal in which they write to respond to each poem at the conclusion of the lesson. • Encourage students to write a poem in response to the poem studied in the lesson. • Challenge students to write in their own voice or in the voice of an imaginary character.

Shell Education is committed to producing educational materials that are research and standards based. In this effort, we have correlated all of our products to the academic standards of all 50 states, the District of Columbia, and the Department of Defense Dependent Schools.

How to Find Standards Correlations

To print a customized correlation report of this product for your state, visit our website at **http://www.shelleducation.com** and follow the on-screen directions. If you require assistance in printing correlation reports, please contact Customer Service at 1-877-777-3450.

Purpose and Intent of Standards

The No Child Left Behind legislation mandates that all states adopt academic standards that identify the skills students will learn in kindergarten through grade twelve. While many states had already adopted academic standards prior to NCLB, the legislation set requirements to ensure the standards were detailed and comprehensive.

Standards are designed to focus instruction and guide adoption of curricula. Standards are statements that describe the criteria necessary for students to meet specific academic goals. They define the knowledge, skills, and content students should acquire at each level. Standards are also used to develop standardized tests to evaluate students' academic progress.

Teachers are required to demonstrate how their lessons meet state standards. State standards are used in development of all of our products, so educators can be assured they meet the academic requirements of each state.

McREL Compendium

We use the Mid-continent Research for Education and Learning (McREL) Compendium to create standards correlations. Each year, McREL analyzes state standards and revises the compendium. By following this procedure, McREL is able to produce a general compilation of national standards. Each lesson in this product is based on one or more McREL standards. The chart on the following pages lists each standard taught in this product and the page number(s) for the corresponding lesson(s).

Standards Correlation Chart

The chart below correlates the activities in *The Poet and the Professor: Poems for Building Reading Skills* with the McREL Content Knowledge.

Standards for Language Arts Grades 6–8

Standards	Benchmarks	Lesson
Uses listening and speaking strategies for different purposes	8.1 Plays a variety of roles in group discussions (e.g., critical listener, discussion leader, facilitator)	All
	8.2 Asks questions to seek elaboration and clarification of ideas	All
	8.4 Listens in order to understand topic, purpose, and perspective in spoken texts (e.g., of a guest speaker, of an informational video, of a televised interview, of radio news programs)	All
	8.7 Uses appropriate verbal and nonverbal techniques for oral presentations (e.g., inflection/modulation of voice, tempo, word choice, grammar, feeling, expression, tone, volume, enunciation, physical gestures, body movement, eye contact, posture)	10, 26
Uses grammatical and mechanical conventions in written compositions	3.1 Uses pronouns in written compositions (e.g., uses relative, demonstrative, personal [i.e., possessive, subject, object] pronouns; uses pronouns that agree with their antecedent)	8, 25
	3.3 Uses verbs in written compositions (e.g., uses linking and auxiliary verbs, verb phrases, and correct forms of regular and irregular verbs)	7, 15, 28
	3.4 Uses adjectives in written compositions (e.g., pronominal, positive, comparative, superlative)	29
	3.6 Uses prepositions and coordinating conjunctions in written compositions (e.g., uses prepositional phrases, combines and embeds ideas using conjunctions)	14, 27
	3.8 Uses conventions of spelling in written compositions (e.g., spells high frequency, commonly misspelled words from appropriate grade-level list; uses a dictionary and other resources to spell words; uses common prefixes, suffixes, and root words as aids to spelling; applies rules for irregular structural changes)	1, 22
	3.9 Uses conventions of capitalization in written compositions (e.g., titles [books, stories, poems, magazines, newspapers, songs, works of art], proper nouns [team names, companies, schools and institutions, departments of government, religions, school subjects], proper adjectives, nationalities, brand names of products)	19, 20
	3.10 Uses conventions of punctuation in written compositions (e.g., uses colons, quotation marks, and dashes; uses apostrophes in contractions and possessives, commas with introductory phrases and dependent clauses, semi-colons or a comma and conjunction in compound sentences, commas in a series)	3
Gathers and uses information for research purposes	4.3 Uses a variety of resource materials to gather information for research topics (e.g., magazines, newspapers, dictionaries, schedules, journals, surveys, globes, atlases, almanacs, websites, databases, podcasts)	16

Standards for Language Arts Grades 6–8 *(cont.)*

Standards	Benchmarks	Lesson
Uses general skills and strategies of the reading process	5.1 Establishes and adjusts purposes for reading (e.g., to understand, interpret, enjoy, solve problems, predict outcomes, answer a specific question, form an opinion, skim for facts; to discover models for own writing)	All
	5.2 Uses word origins and derivations to understand word meaning (e.g., Latin and Greek roots and affixes, meanings of foreign words frequently used in the English language, historical influences on English word meanings)	9, 21
	5.3 Uses a variety of strategies to extend reading vocabulary (e.g., uses analogies, idioms, similes, metaphors to infer the meaning of literal and figurative phrases; uses definition, restatement, example, comparison and contrast to verify word meanings; identifies shades of meaning; knows denotative and connotative meanings; knows vocabulary related to different content areas and current events; uses rhyming dictionaries, classification books, etymological dictionaries)	All
	5.4 Uses specific strategies to clear up confusing parts of text (e.g., pauses, rereads the test, consults another source, represents abstract information as mental pictures, draws upon background knowledge, asks for help)	All
	5.5 Understands specific devices an author uses to accomplish his or her purposes (e.g., persuasive techniques, style, word choice, language structure)	11
	5.6 Reflects on what has been learned after reading and formulates ideas, opinions, and personal responses to texts	24, 30
Uses reading skills and strategies to understand and interpret a variety of literary texts	6.1 Uses reading skills and strategies to understand a variety of literary passages and texts (e.g., fiction, nonfiction, myths, poems, fantasies, biographies, autobiographies, science fiction, drama)	All
	6.3 Understands complex elements of plot development (e.g., cause and effect relationships; use of subplots, parallel episodes, and climax; development of conflict and resolution)	6
	6.10 Makes connections between the motives of characters or the causes for complex events in texts and those in his or her own life	All
Uses reading skills and strategies to understand and interpret a variety of informational texts	7.3 Summarizes and paraphrases information in texts (e.g., arranges information in chronological, logical, or sequential order; conveys main ideas, critical details, and underlying meaning; uses own words or quoted materials; preserves author's perspective and voice)	4, 12, 13
	7.4 Uses new information to adjust and extend personal knowledge base	30
	7.6 Differentiates between fact and opinion in informational texts	2

Activity Skill—Correlation Chart

McREL Content Knowledge Standards for Language Arts Grades 6–8

Activity Page Title	Standards-Based Skill or Focus	Page
Separate It	Syllables (3.8)	20
Feel Free to Disagree	Fact and Opinion (7.6)	24
What Do You Mean?	Differentiating Use of Apostrophe (3.10)	28
Summarize It	Summarizing Text (7.3)	32
Metaphorically Speaking	Metaphors (5.3)	36
Cause and Effect	Cause and Effect (6.3)	40
Past and Present	Verb Tenses (3.3)	44
About Whom Are You Talking?	Pronoun Referents (3.1)	48
They're Related	Word Derivatives (5.2)	52
Sentence Tunes	Fluency—Prosody (8.7)	56
That's an Exaggeration	Author's Device—Exaggeration (5.5)	60
In My Own Words	Sequence and Retell (7.3)	64
It's in the Details	Details (7.3)	68
Transitions	Transitions (3.6)	72
Never, Ever	Double Negatives (3.3)	76
Research and Report	Using Reference Materials (4.3)	80
Means the Same	Synonyms (5.3)	84
Deconstructing Words	Deconstructing Words for Meaning (5.3)	88
Proper Names	Capitalization—Proper Nouns (Names) (3.9)	92
Places and Things	Capitalization—Proper Nouns (Places and Things) (3.9)	96
It's a Noun	Nouns Ending in -sion and -tion (3.3, 5.2)	100
A Different Kind of Division	Syllabication (3.8)	104
Not the Same	Homophones (5.3)	108
This Is Not a Test	Responding to Informational Text (5.6)	112
Replace It	Pronouns (3.1)	116
Vocalize It	Verbal Techniques—Quotations (8.7)	120
Prepositional Phrases	Prepositional Phrases (3.6)	124
Finding Verbs	Identifying Verbs (3.3)	128
Finding Adjectives	Differentiating Adjectives from Adverbs (3.4)	132
Two Sides to Everything	Making Judgments Based on Text (5.6, 7.4)	136

A Chorus of Voices

Although Shaneka, Devin, Alvin, Armando, and Veronica take the credit as the student members of the slam poetry team who contributed their collective works to create this book, the real author is poet Brod Bagert. It is his voice heard in all the poems.

 Encouraged by his teacher, Brod Bagert wrote his first poem in the third grade and has been writing ever since. In high school, his relationship with poetry deepened as he struggled through the love-hate experience of reading the classics in the original Greek and Latin. As a university student, he was intrigued when another student from a neighboring college requested permission to publish two of his poems in her school's poetry review, an experience that led him to discover the power of poetry in the dating ritual.

The world then began to nibble away at Brod's love for poetry. He graduated from law school, married his high-school sweetheart, got elected to public office, and wrote fewer and fewer poems. Then, as a young father, he began to write poems for his own children to recite in their school programs. He was hooked. Deriving less and less satisfaction from a law practice and public career, poetry soon became his full-time occupation.

Brod is now the award-winning author of 17 books of poetry: 10 for children, two for young adults, and five for adults. He is also the author of an Edgar Allan Poe anthology and coauthor of the U.S. Department of Education's *Helping Your Child Learn to Read* (1993). He has appeared at hundreds of conferences, thousands of schools, and has performed his poetry in all 50 states and on five of the world's seven continents.

The heart of Brod's poetry is voice—not just his own voice, but a whole chorus of voices. In a poem for kindergartners, you will hear the voice of a kindergartner; in a poem for classroom teachers, you will hear the voice of a classroom teacher.

Brod's active performance schedule keeps him on the road about half the year. The other half he spends at home in New Orleans. He reads books, rides his bicycle, gardens with his wife, Debby, and dotes on their three rambunctious grandsons.

> *These poems are dedicated to Sue McCoy.*
>
> *—Brod Bagert*

About the Poems

Big, Mean Tween Machine

The poems on which the lessons are based collectively comprise a book of their own—"Big, Mean Tween Machine." The collection begins with an introduction by student Shaneka Byrd, who is the captain of the slam poetry team. Shaneka quickly establishes that she is "The Mouth" and goes on to introduce herself and the rest of the team:

- Shaneka "The Mouth" Byrd
- Devin "I'm-OK-You're-OK" Shay
- Alvin "Nerd-One" Lofton
- Armando "El Fuego" Martí
- Veronica "Queen of the Dead" Page

The team named themselves the Big, Mean Tween Machine because they are sixth graders—somewhere "tween" little kids and teenagers. Their poems reflect the emergence of new emotions, confusion about conflicting feelings, and the discovery of the power of opinion.

The book is divided into five units—one dedicated to each student poet. The introduction sets the stage for the poems in that unit. It gives background about that student and reveals why the given nickname applies. It entices the readers to want to know more about the character, which encourages attentive listening, and allows for immediate understanding and spontaneous audience response. It should also be noted that each of the poems is capable of functioning as a stand-alone piece. This unique style lends itself especially well to reading aloud and involving students in fluency exercises. The format provides built-in flexibility for the teacher and students.

As the introductions and poems are read, it is easy to forget that Shaneka "The Mouth" Byrd and the rest of the students on the "slam poetry" team are all the voice of poet Brod Bagert. He has created five distinct personalities, and in using authentic language and relevant topics, he makes the five members of the Big, Mean Tween Machine seem like real sixth graders.

Introduction

This introduction sets the stage for the entire book. Here we meet the characters who make up the slam poetry team and find out a little about the team itself.

Making Connections

- Help students connect their own experiences to what they are about to read. Ask students to think about times they are together with groups of people—classroom settings, sports, clubs, etc. Have students discuss what types of people make up the various groups. Are the people similar in character or are they completely different? How? Give students time to reflect, and then call on various students to share their thoughts.

- Tell students to listen as you read the introduction to the slam poetry team.

Comprehension Strategy: Critical Thinking—Questioning

- Distribute copies of the introduction or display it for the class.

- Remind students that this introduction sets the stage for the entire set of poems they will be reading. Ask students questions to ensure their understanding of how the slam poetry team came about and who is involved in it. Who is on the team? Who is the leader? What types of poems does the team write?

Standards-Based Skill Focus: Syllables

- Write the word *introduction* on the board. Tell students the word can be broken down into parts or *syllables*. Ask students to say the word *introduction* slowly as they clap for each part of the word (*in-tro-duc-tion*). Tell students that this word has four parts or syllables. Practice with the following words: *slam*, *machine*, *competition*, and *poetry*.

- Provide students practice in separating words into syllables. Distribute copies of the skill activity on page 20. Have students complete the activity individually or in pairs.

Vocabulary Word Study

- Read the first sentence of the introduction to students. Write the words *Byrd* and *bird* on the board. Point out the -*r* controlled spelling in both words. Tell students that learning how to spell *r*-controlled words can be challenging because the sound can be made with the spellings *ir*, *er*, and *ur*.

- Provide students practice in reading and spelling *r*-controlled words. Distribute copies of page 21, which focuses on *r*-controlled words. Complete the activity together as a group if your students seem to need more support with this concept. Otherwise, have students do the activity individually.

Introduction

My name is Shaneka Byrd—pronounced *b-i-r-d* "bird." I'm about to finish sixth grade, and I am our school's slam poetry captain.

I never thought I'd be the kind of person to be involved with poetry, but I love to talk, and the minute Ms. Boltges got us in her library and started talking about a slam poetry team, I knew two things. Number one, I was gonna be on it. And number two, it was gonna be up to me to pull it together. Everybody else knew it, too, so when we had our first meeting, I just took over, and that was that. Now don't get me wrong. My teammates are not wimps. They just all wanted the best for the team, and that was me. I'm not claiming to be the best poet, just the best leader. It's my gift.

There were five of us on this year's team:

Yours truly, Shaneka "The Mouth" Byrd

Devin "I'm-OK-You're-OK" Shay

Alvin "Nerd-One" Lofton

Armando "El Fuego" Martí and

Veronica "Queen of the Dead" Page

We called ourselves "The Big, Mean Tween Machine," and we finished third in the state competition, which made us all happy, except I still think we should have been number one. This book is a collection of our poems. We had a lot of fun with these poems, both writing them and performing them. We entertained a lot of people, especially our own classmates; and now, with this book, we hope to entertain you.

By the way, we did not write these poems in sweet little whispers. We wrote them to produce over-the-top, in-your-face, tell-it-like-it-is, blow-it-out performances, which is how we performed them. But we can't be in your classroom, so we're counting on you to make it happen. Just find a poem you really like, practice acting it out, get up in front of your class, and do it. You're gonna be great.

Name: _____

Separate It

I. Directions: Divide the words into syllables using hyphens.

1. pronounced _____

2. captain _____

3. involved _____

4. competition _____

5. collection _____

6. entertained _____

7. practice _____

8. classroom _____

9. performances _____

10. whispers _____

• •

II. Directions: Read each sentence below. Choose from the words above to complete the sentence. Write the correct word on the line.

11. The goal was kicked by the _____ of the team.

12. Mrs. Glisbury has a stamp _____.

13. The magician _____ us with his magic act.

14. He is _____ in many activities after school.

15. The _____ in the spelling bee was fierce.

Name:_____

Introduction

I. Directions: Sort the words below in the correct column.

| entertained | thirteen | giraffe | chirp | sir |
| sister | thunder | circus | yesterday | ruler |

ir Words	*er* Words

• •

II. Directions: Use the words above to answer each riddle.

1. I am something you measure with. _____

2. I am the opposite of tomorrow. _____

3. I am a place with clowns and elephants. _____

4. I am the sound a bird makes. _____

5. I occur after lightning. _____

Extension

Write riddles for the other five words that were not used in section II.

Shaneka "The Mouth" Byrd

This mini biography of Shaneka tells a lot about her in just a few short paragraphs. It sets the stage for her poems that will follow. In it, we learn why Shaneka is "The Mouth."

Making Connections

- Help students connect their own experiences to what they are about to read. Ask students to think about these questions: What information would you share with others about yourself? How would you describe your personality? Do you have parts of your personality that you like? That you dislike? Give students time to reflect, and then call on various students to share their thoughts.

- Tell students to listen as you read "Shaneka 'The Mouth' Byrd."

Comprehension Strategy: Critical Thinking—Analysis

- Distribute copies of Shaneka's introduction or display it for the class.

- Remind students that Shaneka describes herself in this introduction. What does Shaneka say that she *is*? What does she say she *is not*? Why does she describe herself as "The Mouth"? How did she gain favor with her classmates? Have students use evidence from Shaneka's introduction to support their answers.

Standards-Based Skill Focus: Fact and Opinion

- Remind students that a *fact* is a statement that is true and can be proven. An *opinion* is someone's personal feelings, ideas, and beliefs. Give these examples. Fact: Roses are a type of flower. Opinion: Roses are the prettiest flowers.

- Review the information Shaneka shares about herself in "Shaneka 'The Mouth' Byrd" and decide as a class which sentences are facts and which are opinions.

- Distribute copies of the skill activity on page 24. Have students complete the activity individually or in pairs.

Vocabulary Word Study

- Tell students that a good way to find opinions is to recognize and use words that signal opinions. Distribute copies of page 25, which focuses on opinion words. First, explain that certain words signal that a statement is an opinion. Some of these appear in the list on the page. Read through the words together, stopping to discuss how or why they might alert a reader that a statement is an opinion rather than a fact.

- Complete the activity together as a group if your students seem to need more support with this concept. Otherwise, have students do the activity individually.

Shaneka 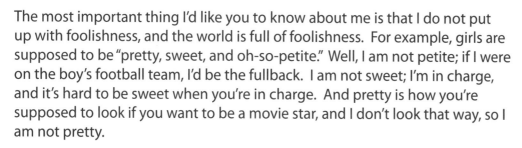 Byrd

I've got two little brothers and a baby sister. I've been taking care of them all my life, so for me, being in charge comes natural. That's why I'm captain of our school's slam poetry team. But being in charge doesn't mean you get to tell everybody else what to do. The very last thing I want is to steamroll my teammates. I expect every member of our team to carry their own weight. If one of us needs help, we are all there for each other. But if one of us gets lazy, I will deal with that myself.

The most important thing I'd like you to know about me is that I do not put up with foolishness, and the world is full of foolishness. For example, girls are supposed to be "pretty, sweet, and oh-so-petite." Well, I am not petite; if I were on the boy's football team, I'd be the fullback. I am not sweet; I'm in charge, and it's hard to be sweet when you're in charge. And pretty is how you're supposed to look if you want to be a movie star, and I don't look that way, so I am not pretty.

Now that I've told you what I'm not; let me tell you what I am. I'm strong. I'm not just physically strong. I'm emotionally and intellectually and morally strong, and I use that strength to stand up for people who may not be as strong as me. It's not like I'm a real nice person, it's just that I can't stand by and watch somebody get pushed around. I know what it feels like to be pushed around, and I'm not about to let it happen to somebody else, not if I can help it.

Now, that's the easy part; here comes the hard part. It's hard to explain. I don't really understand it myself, but deep down inside, I feel like it's my job to speak for everybody around me, like we're all part of one body, and I'm the mouth. You'll see what I mean when you read my poem "Big! Mean! Tween! Machine!" When I wrote that poem, our whole class was feeling the same way, like we were all starting to grow up, but they were still treatin' us like little kids. Everybody was feeling it, but nobody was saying anything about it, so I put it in a poem. You should have been there the first time I performed it. I got up in front of the whole class, I gave a kind of in-your-face smile, and then, in the strongest voice I could find, I said the title—"BIG! MEAN! TWEEN! MACHINE!" And on each word I jabbed my finger like the back wall of the classroom was the whole grown-up world, and then, when I recited the poem, I just let-'em-have-it. At the end I took a bow, and everybody clapped. There were even a few cheers, and that made me feel real good, like I was doing what I was meant to do, because that's what I am. The Mouth. And I love what I am, which makes me an extremely beautiful human being.

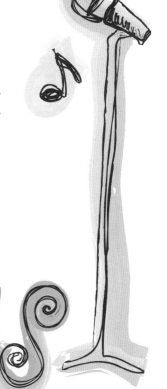

Name: _____

Feel Free to Disagree

Directions: A *fact* is something that is true and can be proven. An *opinion* is what a person thinks, feels, or believes. Read each statement about pets. Write *F* on the line if it is a fact. Write *O* if it is an opinion.

_____ 1. Dogs and cats are the most common household pets.

_____ 2. Cats are easier to take care of than dogs.

_____ 3. Goldfish are the best pets because they can live up to 40 years.

_____ 4. Before getting a pet, you ought to consider how much space the pet needs.

_____ 5. It is hard to teach a dog tricks.

_____ 6. Most cats have five toes on their front feet but only four on their back feet.

_____ 7. Everyone enjoys having a pet around the house.

_____ 8. Having a pet snake is dangerous.

_____ 9. Cats and dogs should not live in the same home.

_____ 10. February is Pet Dental Health Awareness month.

_____ 11. If you have a dog, you must be aware of things that might be poisonous to it.

_____ 12. It would be fun to teach a parrot to talk.

_____ 13. It is illegal to keep certain animals as pets.

_____ 14. Pets usually are considered part of the family.

_____ 15. Empty paper towel rolls and empty boxes make great toys for all cats.

_____ 16. Puppies and kittens have different dietary needs from their adult counterparts.

Name: _____

Shaneka "The Mouth" Byrd

Directions: Find and underline the word or words in each sentence that signal that the statement may be an opinion. For an extra challenge, use a book or sheet of paper to cover the list as you work.

Opinion Words

should	shouldn't	certain	may	believe
worst	seems	extremely	good	better
important	rather	hard	probably	too much

1. Being twelve is better than being eleven.

2. Ms. Jarrel gives too much homework!

3. You should have breakfast before coming to school.

4. Karen is probably mad about coming in second place.

5. That was the worst pizza I've ever had.

6. Terra has good ideas.

7. I am certain that Mom will say yes.

8. You are good at sports.

9. It's hard to keep quiet when I disagree with someone.

10. Paul would rather read than watch a movie.

11. There may be life on distant planets.

12. Speaking in front of the class makes me extremely nervous.

13. Getting regular dental checkups is important for your health.

14. My dog seems to know what time it is.

15. I believe that either team can win any given game.

16. You shouldn't be afraid to try new things.

Extension

Write two facts and two opinions about yourself. Label each statement as fact or opinion.

Big! Mean! Tween! Machine!

Here, Shaneka gives us our first look into her personality as she writes about her upcoming twelfth birthday.

Making Connections

- Help students connect their own experiences to what they are about to read. Ask students to think about these questions: What comes to your mind when someone tells another person to *grow up*? What's the difference between *grown-up* and *all grown-up*? In what ways are you grown-up and not so grown-up? Give students time to reflect, and then call on various students to share their thoughts.

- Tell students to listen as you read Shaneka's poem about her upcoming twelfth birthday.

Comprehension Strategy: Making Inferences

- Distribute copies of the poem or display it for the class.

- Explain that it is sometimes necessary to "read between the lines" or figure out information that is not directly stated in the text. Ask the following questions, and have students give evidence from the poem that supports their answers: How can you tell that Shaneka has known Julian for a long time? Who is Shaneka talking to when she asks for a little respect? What do you think *tween* means?

Standards-Based Skill Focus: Differentiating Use of Apostrophe

- Ask students to underline or highlight the following words in the poem: *birthday's, I'm, twelve's, it's, don't, we're,* and *future's.* Point out that the apostrophe in each word takes the place of one or more letters. Ask students to identify the two words from which each was shortened (birthday is, I am, twelve is, it is, do not, we are, future is).

- Have students complete the skill activity on individual copies of page 28.

Vocabulary Word Study

- Distribute copies of page 29. Point out that all the words in the first section are number words—the written form of a numeral. Teach these rules for using number words: 1. Spell out the numbers from *one* to *one hundred.* Use numerals for 101 and up. (Note: Newspapers and some other texts use numerals for 10 and up.) 2. Use hyphens in number words *twenty-one* through *ninety-nine.* 3. Never use *and* as part of a number word (e.g., 308 should be three hundred eight).

- Have students complete the word study activity individually or with partners.

Big! Mean! Tween! Machine!

by Shaneka Byrd

My birthday's next week.
I'm turning twelve,
and I know that twelve's not "all grown up,"
but it's close.
And things are starting to change,
like the way I feel about boys—

    I still don't actually like boys,
    but when Julian Buckley smiles at me,
    it doesn't make me want to puke anymore.

And it's not just me,
it's happening to all my friends,
even the boys;
we are all growing up.

And I know—
with grown-up feelings
come grown-up responsibilities,
but we're ready to take that on, too,
which is why I think it's time we get
a little more of your respect.

So ready or not! Here we come!
Young and strong and lean!
Next week the future's turning twelve—
Big! Mean! Tween! Machine!

Name: _____

What Do You Mean?

Directions: Each sentence below has a word that contains an apostrophe ('). The apostrophe stands for one or more letters taken out of two words to form the shortened word. Next to each sentence, write the two words from which the bold word was formed.

1. My **birthday's** next week. _____ _____

2. I know that **twelve's** not grown up. _____ _____

3. No, but **it's** getting there. _____ _____

4. It **doesn't** mean that I am done growing. _____ _____

5. I **don't** have to give up my friends. _____ _____

6. **We're** all growing up together! _____ _____

7. We are still young, but the **future's** ours. _____ _____

8. I guess **I'm** really a tween. _____ _____

9. **That's** just fine with me. _____ _____

10. **I'd** rather take my time at this growing up. _____ _____

11. **There's** one kid thing I want to do. _____ _____

12. Being all grown up—**it'll** come soon enough. _____ _____

Name:_____

Big! Mean! Tween! Machine!

I. Directions: Write the numeral that corresponds to each number word below.

ninety _____	fourteen _____	thirty-five _____
ten _____	fifty-six _____	sixty-three _____
forty _____	thirteen _____	two _____
fifteen _____	eighty-one _____	twenty-nine _____
ten _____	seventy _____	one hundred _____
eighty _____	eighteen _____	seventy-five _____
zero _____	nineteen _____	one thousand _____
sixty _____	seventeen _____	twenty-four _____

II. Directions: Write the number words for each numeral below.

1. 12 _____

2. 110 _____

3. 39 _____

4. 40,000 _____

5. 22 _____

6. 800 _____

7. 94 _____

8. 1,000,000 _____

9. 73 _____

10. 601 _____

Extension

Think of three ways that being 12 is different from being 11. Write to explain.

Denied

Shaneka's second poem tells about a recent experience she had at the mall. In her poem, "Denied," Shaneka shares her feelings about what happened.

Making Connections

- Help students connect their own experiences to what they are about to read. Ask students to think about a time they were denied something that they really wanted. Allow time for students to think and then have several students share their thoughts or experiences with the class.

- Tell students that they will listen to a poem about a girl who does not get what she wants. Ask students to listen to what it is she wants and what she does not get as you read the poem aloud.

Comprehension Strategy: Text-to-Self Connections

- Distribute copies of the poem or display it for the class.

- Tell students that one way to gain a deeper understanding of a text is to make a text-to-self connection. These connections are made when the text reminds you of a similar experience, feeling, or event. Help students make text-to-self connections by asking them these questions about themselves and the text: Where do you like to hang out with your friends? Where were these friends hanging out? Have your feelings toward another person ever changed? How did the person's feelings in the poem change?

Standards-Based Skill Focus: Summarizing Text

- Tell students that a good way to check for understanding is to summarize events that happened. One way to do this with a short passage such as a poem is to summarize each stanza.

- Distribute copies of page 32. Have a student read aloud the first stanza. Demonstrate how these four lines could be summarized in one sentence, such as *Jeremy and I sort of liked to be with each other.* Model how to write the summary sentence next to the first stanza. Then repeat the same procedure with the other stanzas.

- Have students read the summary sentences together. Ask students if the four-sentence summary provides the gist of the poem. Why or why not?

Vocabulary Word Study

- Have students highlight the lines of the poem that end with rhyming words. Students should identify that the last word in the second and fourth lines of each stanza rhyme.

- Distribute page 33, which focuses on finding and creating words that rhyme with the words that rhyme in the poem. Review the directions together and then allow students to complete the activity in pairs or individually.

Denied

by Shaneka Byrd

Jeremy and I were not dating,
which was plain enough to see,
but I liked to be around him
and he liked to be with me.

But yesterday at the mall,
he was acting really vague.
You'd have thought he didn't know me.
You'd have thought I had the plague.

And when his friends came up to us,
he almost tried to hide me.
I can't believe that dirty rat
just stood there and denied me.

Now every time I think of him,
I feel a little chill.
Oh no, I never dated him.
And now? I never will!

Name:_____

Summarize It

Directions: Read each stanza from the poem "Denied." Write a one-sentence summary in the box next to the stanza. When you are done, read aloud all the summary sentences together to summarize the entire poem.

Poem	Summary
Jeremy and I were not dating, which was plain enough to see, but I liked to be around him and he liked to be with me.	_____ _____ _____
But yesterday at the mall, he was acting really vague. You'd have thought he didn't know me. You'd have thought I had the plague.	_____ _____ _____
And when his friends came up to us, he almost tried to hide me. I can't believe that dirty rat just stood there and denied me.	_____ _____ _____
Now every time I think of him, I feel a little chill. Oh no, I never dated him. And now? I never will!	_____ _____

Name:_____

Denied

Directions: The words on the chart below are rhyming words from the poem "Denied." Write the words that rhyme in the correct column. Then think of two more words that rhyme and write them in each column. Finally, answer the questions at the bottom.

Italy	fulfill	Brazil	guarantee	spill
degree	debris	refill	disagree	until

	me and see	chill and will
Word Bank Rhyming Words	_____ _____ _____ _____ _____ _____	_____ _____ _____ _____ _____ _____
New Rhyming Words	_____ _____	_____ _____

1. Do words that rhyme have to have the same spelling patterns at the ends of the words?

   _____

2. Why do you think there was not a column for words that rhyme with *vague* and *plague*?

   _____

Extension

Think of two other pairs of words that rhyme but do not have the same spelling pattern.

Hurricane Henrietta

This poem by Shaneka vividly describes a classmate who likes to be at the center of the action. Shaneka names the classmate "Hurricane Henrietta" because she stirs up a storm of trouble and can strike at any time.

Making Connections

- Help students connect their own experiences to what they are about to read. Ask students to think about someone they know who "tells stories" about others just to stir up trouble. Then ask volunteers to offer reasons why they think a person might do that.

- Tell students that they will listen to a poem about a girl who makes up stories about people just to get attention. Ask students to listen for different ways Shaneka describes Henrietta. Have students listen as you read the poem aloud.

Comprehension Strategy: Clarify

- Distribute copies of the poem or display it for the class.

- Help students clarify their understanding by discussing these questions: What does Shaneka mean by *making sweet eyes*? What does it mean when Shaneka says that Henrietta is *at it again*? What does Shaneka mean by saying that you never know when *Henrietta's going to strike*? Why does Shaneka call her *Hurricane Henrietta*?

Standards-Based Skill Focus: Metaphors

- Tell students that a good way to describe something is to compare it to something else. A *metaphor* is a direct comparison— a description that compares, as if one thing actually were another thing, not just like it. Offer these examples from the poem: *Henrietta Brinks is a natural disaster* (not just like one); *to stir up a storm of angry feelings* (the feelings are a storm, not just like one).

- Distribute copies of page 36. To ensure that students learn the concept, you may want to complete the activity together.

Vocabulary Word Study

- Distribute copies of page 37, which focuses on weather words (and their function as metaphors as well as their overt meanings).

- Tell students that a good way to increase vocabulary is by learning words in categories. Call on students to read the words from the box and tell their meanings. Clarify meanings as needed. Then have students complete the word study activity individually.

Hurricane Henrietta

by Shaneka Byrd

Yesterday she looked me right in the eye
and told me how my friend Alma was a tramp.
So I said, "Henrietta, just stop it."
And I walked away.

Well, Henrietta didn't like that,
so the next thing I knew
she was telling my friend Fiona
about how she saw me making sweet eyes
at Fiona's boyfriend, Marcus.
And Fiona almost believed her.
Then she thought,
Shaneka Byrd has never made sweet eyes in her life,
and she realized Henrietta was at it again.

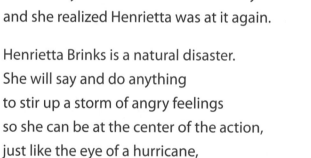

Marcus

Henrietta Brinks is a natural disaster.
She will say and do anything
to stir up a storm of angry feelings
so she can be at the center of the action,
just like the eye of a hurricane,
which is why I call her Hurricane Henrietta.

But we get warnings about most natural disasters.
They warn us about hurricanes,
they warn us about tornadoes,
they even tell us when a volcano's about to erupt,
but there's no such thing as a Henrietta warning.

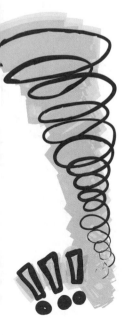

So at school we live with a constant threat,
both girls and boys alike,
the threat that any second
Henrietta's going to strike.

Name: _____

Metaphorically Speaking

Directions: Each description below contains a metaphor. Find and underline the metaphor. Then write what it means on the line.

1. If I am late, I am a lobster in hot water.

   _____

2. Mom declared my room a disaster area.

   _____

3. My big brother is a pig when it comes to eating pizza.

   _____

4. The show about pet training was food for thought.

   _____

5. The news was music to my ears.

   _____

6. The homework assignment was a breeze.

   _____

Name:_____

Hurricane Henrietta

I. Directions: Read the words in the box below. Discuss the meaning(s) for each word with your class. Hint: Some words may have more than one meaning.

barometer	blizzard	breeze	chill	cloudy	cold
drizzle	flood	foggy	freeze	frost	hail
hot	humid	hurricane	ice	lightning	mist
overcast	rain	showers	sleet	slush	smog
sprinkle	storm	sunny	thunder	tornado	typhoon

II. Directions: Read each sentence below. Decide if the weather word is meant to have its actual meaning or is being used as a metaphor. Put a ✓ in the column of your choice.

Actual   Metaphor

_____   _____   **1.** Henrietta is a hurricane that could strike at any time.

_____   _____   **2.** The forecast was for drizzle in the morning.

_____   _____   **3.** When my best friend moved away, I felt a flood of emotions.

_____   _____   **4.** Dad says that I have a sunny disposition.

_____   _____   **5.** The pictures didn't come out well because it was overcast.

_____   _____   **6.** When I woke up this morning, my mind was foggy.

_____   _____   **7.** That basketball player is lightning on the court.

_____   _____   **8.** Snow and sleet caused three car accidents this week.

Extension

Describe how you would handle it if someone told untrue stories about you.

Big Sister

In her final contribution in the collection of poems by the slam poetry team, Shaneka turns her attention toward her younger brother. Here, as in her other poems, she asserts her self-proclaimed authority.

Making Connections

- Help students connect their own experiences to what they are about to read. Ask students to consider whether there should be different rules and standards for children based on age. For example, should an older child in a family get more privileges than a younger one? Should an older child have authority over a younger one? Lead a class discussion.

- Introduce the term *double standard* as a rule or expectation that is applied unfairly so that what is acceptable for one person is not acceptable for another.

- Ask students to listen for an example of a double standard as you read Shaneka's poem about her younger brother. (Shaneka's view of censorship in the final stanza is a double standard.)

Comprehension Strategy: Imagery

- Distribute copies of the poem or display it for the class.

- Explain that writers carefully select phrases to create images in readers' minds. Ask students to identify examples of this in the poem. Ask students the following questions: Instead of saying her brother's poem made her mad, how did Shaneka describe her anger? (*my hands began to tremble with rage; foam trickled from the corners of my mouth*) Instead of saying she would get back at him, what did she say she would do? (*steal his teddy bear and tear off both its arms*)

Standards-Based Skill Focus: Cause and Effect

- Create a two-column chart on the board. Label one column *cause* and the other column *effect*. Explain that *cause* is the reason for something and *effect* is the result.

- Give this example from the poem: Cause: Shaneka's brother wrote a poem about her. Effect: Shaneka got angry. Record the cause and effect on the chart. Challenge students to find another example of cause and effect in the poem. (Cause: Shaneka put him in his place. Effect: He writes only drippy-sweet poems.)

- Have students complete the skill activity on individual copies of page 40.

Vocabulary Word Study

- Write these words from the poem on the board: *little*, *tremble*, *trickled*, and *terrible*. Ask students if they noticed that all the words have the spelling pattern *–le*. Tell students other words are spelled with the *-el* spelling pattern. Emphasize to students that they must learn which words use which spelling pattern.

- Distribute copies of page 41 to students. Review the directions and then have students complete the page independently.

BIG SISTER

by Shaneka Byrd

My little brother wrote his first poem.

> Sister! Sister! Missy-miss!
> Met a boy she had to kiss.
> His face turned green. His skin turned gray.
> He shouted YUCK! and ran away.

And he didn't just say it.
Oh no.
It was over, and over, and over again
'til my hands began to tremble with rage,
and foam trickled from the corners of my mouth.

That's when I decided
to compose a poem of my own.

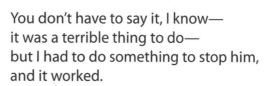

> Clever, clever little brother,
> he writes poetic charms.
> Next time I'll steal his teddy bear
> and tear off both its arms.

You don't have to say it, I know—
it was a terrible thing to do—
but I had to do something to stop him,
and it worked.

'Cause now his poems are drippy-sweet
with flattery and grace.
That dose of sister censorship
just put him in his place.

So censorship is not so bad,
as you can plainly see,
as long as no one out there EVER
tries to censor me.

Name:_____

Cause and Effect

Directions: The column on the left contains the first part of a sentence and describes the cause, or reason, for something. The column on the right contains the effect, or result, of each thing, but not in the correct order. Match each effect to its cause by drawing a line.

CAUSE	EFFECT
1. Jason didn't arrive at the bus stop on time,	therefore school was canceled.
2. It snowed overnight;	I didn't invite her to my party.
3. Since Jen was ignoring me	so the bus left without him.
4. Because someone left the water in the tub running,	the factory cut its production.
5. Due to a slowdown in demand for new cars,	resulted in him getting an infection.
6. So many people showed up	the water overflowed onto the floor.
7. The vet said that a cut on my dog's paw	that there was not room for everyone.
8. If we don't complete an assignment in class,	so I ended up having to pay a fine.
9. I forgot to return my library books,	Dad gets annoyed and makes me turn it down.
10. When I play my music loudly,	then we have to finish it for homework.

Name: _____

Big Sister

Directions: The answer to each clue is a word that is missing just two letters—an *l* and an e. However, in order to spell the word correctly, you must know in which order they come: *-le* or *-el*. Fill in the missing letters in the correct order.

1. small: l i t t __ __

2. to shake or quiver: t r e m b __ __

3. awful or dreadful: t e r r i b __ __

4. a five-cent coin: n i c k __ __

5. two times: d o u b __ __

6. eat in tiny bites: n i b b __ __

7. to laugh quietly: g i g g __ __

8. to stop or reverse: c a n c __ __

9. an animal with humps: c a m __ __

10. one, all by itself: s i n g __ __

11. a heavenly being: a n g __ __

12. a flat surface with legs: t a b __ __

13. a grade or flat surface: l e v __ __

14. to flow slowly in a stream: t r i c k __ __

15. place to sleep overnight: h o t __ __

16. to go to another place: t r a v __ __

17. molded wax used for light: c a n d __ __

18. a heavy round bread roll: b a g __ __

19. used with thread to sew: n e e d __ __

20. able or likely to happen: p o s s i b __ __

21. location of a TV signal: c h a n n __ __

22. short informational text: a r t i c __ __

23. a fight between two people: d u __ __

24. an attachment to identify: l a b __ __

Extension

How confident were you in your spelling choices above? Predict how many you spelled correctly out of all 24. Then use a dictionary to verify the spellings and see how close your prediction was.

Devin "I'm-OK-You're-OK" Shay

Devin is the next of the slam poetry team to contribute poems. Before we read his poems, the team's captain, Shaneka, provides a glimpse into Devin's personality.

Making Connections

- Help students connect their own experiences to what they are about to read. Ask students to think of a time they have had a difference of opinion with a peer. How did you handle it? Did you confront the person? Give students time to reflect and then ask a few volunteers to share their thoughts.

- Tell students that they will listen to Shaneka's introduction of Devin, another student in her poetry group. Ask students to focus on how Shaneka describes Devin. Have students listen as you read the introduction aloud.

Comprehension Strategy: Problem and Solution

- Distribute copies of Shaneka's introduction of Devin or display it for the class.

- Remind students that Devin is described as "I'm-OK-You're-OK" Shay. Ask students to find evidence in the introduction that supports this nickname.

- Have students identify the problem Shaneka has with Devin. Ask students to identify how Devin tries to solve the problem at first. Ask students to identify how Devin solves the problem once Shaneka asks for the truth.

- Write the two different solutions to the problem on the board. Ask students to discuss why Devin tried the first solution. How does that fit with his personality? Ask students which solution they would prefer.

Standards-Based Skill Focus: Verb Tenses

- Use Devin's introduction as a springboard for reviewing verb tense. Remind students that present tense means that the action is happening now, or in the present. Past tense means that action happened before, or in the past.

- On the board, draw two columns and label them *present* and *past*. Write the words *explain* and *explained* in the correct columns and tell why you are doing so. Say, "Today, Devin will explain why the poem is rotten. Yesterday, he *explained* why the poem was rotten." Continue this sentence pattern with a few more verbs from the introduction.

- Distribute copies of page 44. Have students use the clues to find present and past tense verbs to complete the crossword puzzle. Allow students to work in pairs if necessary.

Vocabulary Word Study

- Tell students that words can not only describe things, but they can also create images in our minds. Ask students what or whom they think of when you say the following words: *bossy*, *kind*, *angry*, *fearful*, and *caring*.

- Distribute page 45 to students. Tell students to think about Devin's introduction and what kind of person he is. Then tell them to follow the directions to create a picture with words (and with a drawing) of his character.

Devin Shay
I'M-OK-YOU'RE-OK

A couple of the girls in our class are interested in boys, but most of us couldn't care less, except when it comes to Devin Shay. At one time or another, every girl in school has had a thing for Devin, which is really funny because Devin gets so nervous around girls, you'd think he was gonna be sick.

Devin Shay lives a charmed life. He's good at everything he does, everybody likes him, and he's so cute it's disgusting. He's also smart, athletic, funny, talented, and such a nice person it makes you feel guilty when you realize that you're jealous of him.

Some of our friends think Devin's a little light upstairs. Well, during our slam thing, I really got to know him, and I can tell you that Devin Shay is anything but "light upstairs." He's just always trying to avoid conflict. It's not like he's afraid; it's more like he's polite. I think, deep down, he knows that life has dealt him a pretty good hand, and that makes him reluctant to elbow us "less fortunates" around.

Here's an example. I had written this really rotten poem, but when I showed it to Devin, he started telling me how cool it was. Now I knew it wasn't cool, and I knew he knew it wasn't cool, which is when I decided to get up in his face. "Dude!" I said. "Don't tell me what you think I want to hear. I'm your friend, and when I ask for your opinion, I deserve the truth."

"You're right," he said. "You do deserve the truth." Then he told me my poem didn't work and explained exactly why it didn't work. It may have been the best writing lesson I ever got.

So Devin is not light upstairs. He just wants to get along with everybody; and he avoids conflict, ends up with a pile of friends, and isn't really close to any of them. He's good at everything he does, so I'm pretty sure he'll be successful no matter what, but if Devin Shay ever decides to stand up for what he believes, he's the kind of person who just might make the world a better place.

Name:_____

Past and Present

Directions: Each clue below is a verb in "Devin 'I'm-OK-You're-OK' Shay." Solve the puzzle by using the clues below. Be careful! Some of these are tricky!

Down

1. past tense of *show*

2. present tense of *thought*

4. present tense of *realized*

5. present tense of *made*

7. past tense of *deal*

Across

3. past tense of *tell*

6. past tense of *explain*

8. past tense of *start*

9. present tense of *told*

10. past tense of *know*

Name:_____

Devin "I'm-OK-You're-OK" Shay

I. Directions: In Shaneka's introduction, you met Devin. Now, it is your turn to respond to what you read. Read the list of traits below. Circle all those that you think describe Devin well. Cross out any that definitely do not describe him. Use a dictionary to look up any words you do not know. Try to only use the words that accurately describe him.

cautious	critical	fearful	polite
hopeful	amusing	genuine	bossy
honorable	smart	calm	respectful
rebellious	feisty	loyal	accepting
indifferent	reluctant	nervous	arrogant

II. Directions: In the box below, sketch a picture of how you imagine Devin "I'm-OK-You're-OK" Shay looks and dresses.

Extension

Think about Devin. Would you like Devin as a friend? Why or why not?

Rude Dude

In this poem, Devin is short and to the point as he writes about someone who ignored him.

Making Connections

- Help students connect their own experiences to what they are about to read. Ask students what it means to be rude.

- Have students think of a time when they noticed someone being rude. Then ask a few volunteers to share their thoughts and experiences. Remind them to talk about the experience without naming particular people. Offer a simple example, such as "Once someone used something of mine without asking permission."

- Tell students that they will listen to a poem in which Devin describes a "rude dude." Have students listen as you read the poem aloud. Then ask students what action Devin thought was rude and how he felt about it.

Comprehension Strategy: Literary Terms—Irony

- Distribute copies of the poem or display it for the class.

- Write the term *irony* on the board. Ask if anyone can explain its meaning. Accept any answers without comment, and then read this definition: something that happens that has an unexpected or surprising result—especially when it is funny or amusing.

- Challenge students to explain how Devin's poem uses irony.

Standards-Based Skill Focus: Pronoun Referents

- Remind students that words such as *she, he, it, I, me, you, we, us, each, both, them,* and *they* are called *pronouns* and take the place of the names of people, places, or things.

- Have a volunteer read the first stanza of the poem aloud. Have students highlight the words *I, you'll, him, he, his,* and *me* in the poem. Ask them to identify whom Devin is talking about (*I*—Devin; *you'll*—the reader; *him, he, his*—the Rude Dude; and *me*—Devin).

- Ask students to identify the pronouns in the second stanza of the poem. Discuss what noun/name each pronoun refers to.

- Distribute copies of page 48 for students to complete individually or with a partner.

Vocabulary Word Study

- Remind students that some words have silent letters.

- Distribute copies of page 49. Have students write in the missing letters from a variety of words with silent letters. Before they start, make sure any copies of the poem are out of sight. When they are done with the activity, review the answers together as a group.

Rude!! Dude

by Devin Shay

That dude was very rude,
I know you'll all agree.
Right when I tried to talk to him,
he turned his back on me.

So I just watched him walk away,
he never looked around,
and now I guess he'll never know,
he left his zipper down.

Name: _____

About Whom Are You Talking?

Directions: Each sentence below contains one or more pronouns. Write what each bold word refers to or means. For example, in the sentence *Shaneka thinks that she'll win*, she'll = she will, meaning Shaneka will, so she'll = Shaneka will.

1. Devin and Shaneka were **both** busy writing new poems for the contest.

   both = _____

2. Devin was writing about the Rude Dude **he** met in the hall earlier.

   he = _____

3. Devin said to Rude Dude, "**You** had better hurry up. The bell is about to ring."

   You = _____

4. Shaneka didn't even look up at the time. **She** didn't care about **it**.

   She = _____ it = _____

5. "Well, **I** am done," said Devin. "**My** poem is short, but really good."

   I = _____ My = _____

6. "**I** am sure **it** is," said Shaneka. "But **mine** will win the contest."

   I = _____ it = _____

   mine = _____

7. "**We'll** see about that," said Devin. "**I'll** wait for the judges. **Their** opinion is the only **one** that counts!"

   We'll = _____ I'll = _____

   Their = _____ one = _____

Name: _____

Rude Dude

Directions: You have seen all of the bold words below many, many times. The question is how well did you really see the words? Test your observation and memory skills. Fill in the missing letter(s) from each word. **Hint:** The missing letter is silent in that word.

1. It is always fun to visit with my **a____nt** and uncle.

2. Devin always tries to do the **ri___ ___t** thing.

3. Murray asked me to **wa___ch** his bike while he went into the store.

4. I have to **wa___k** our dog every morning and evening.

5. Jenny invited me to **lis___en** to the new music she downloaded.

6. This year, my birthday falls on a **We___nesday**.

7. Valentine's Day is always on **Feb___uary** 14.

8. For good dental health, you should see the dentist **of___en**.

9. I got the letter, but I haven't had time to **ans___er** it yet.

10. The ship dropped anchor just off the coast of a little **i___land**.

11. I like learning to play the piano, but I wish I **cou___d** learn faster!

12. My favorite ice cream flavor is chocolate **fu___ge** swirl.

Extension

Think about the word *rude*. Write the list of words below. Then, next to each word, write *synonym* if it means the same or almost the same or *antonym* if it means the opposite. Word list: *impolite, mannerly, gracious, discourteous, ill-mannered, courteous.*

Sisters and Brothers

In his second poem, Devin is frustrated of having his innocent actions misinterpreted.

Making Connections

- Help students connect their own experiences to what they are about to read. Ask students to think of a time when they or someone they know "took something the wrong way."

- Write the term *misinterpret* on the board. Ask students what they think it means. After allowing several responses, ask a few volunteers to share their experiences with misinterpreting someone's words or actions.

- Tell students that they will listen to a poem in which Devin explains how something he did was misinterpreted. Have students listen as you read the poem aloud.

Comprehension Strategy: Author's Word Choice

- Distribute copies of the poem or display it for the class.

- Explain that Devin's poem uses expressions that are not commonly used in formal writing. Doing this helps Devin seem like a "real" sixth grader talking to other sixth graders like him.

- Ask by a show of hands who has ever heard or used the following expressions: *here's the thing*, describing someone as a *rat*, calling something that's fake as *bogus*, and *talking trash*. Invite students to explain the meanings of these expressions in the poem.

Standards-Based Skill Focus: Word Derivatives

- Tell students that many words are just different forms of a single word. If they learn one word, they may more easily be able to figure out several others that are derived from it. Say, "For example, if you know the word *offend* as meaning hurting someone's feelings or breaking the law, you can figure out *offending*, *offense*, *offensive*, and *offender*."

- Distribute copies of page 52. Have students complete the activity individually or in pairs.

Vocabulary Word Study

- Provide practice in finding and correcting commonly misspelled words—an ongoing and important part of word study.

- Distribute copies of page 53. Have students proofread sentences for spelling errors and correct the mistakes. Before they start, make sure any copies of the poem are out of sight.

SISTERS AND BROTHERS

by Devin Shay

There's this girl named Shanell Harrison.
She goes to our school,
and last week she wrote a poem about me:

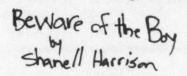

Beware of the Boy
by Shanell Harrison

I thought he really liked me.
I thought we'd never part.
I thought I was the girl of his dreams,
but then he broke my heart.

So hear me, all my sisters,
and remember what I say:
protect yourselves from lying boys
like lowdown Devin Shay.

Shanell

Devin

That's what she wrote,
but here's the thing—

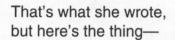

Fig. 1

in my whole life I've never had a girlfriend,
Shanell Harrison or anybody else.
But last week in the cafeteria
Shanell sat next to me,
and I was nice to her.
And I wouldn't even care what she wrote
except that every girl in school
is saying what a rat I am
for breaking Shanell Harrison's heart.

Fig 2

I'm absolutely innocent,
it's a totally bogus offense,
but when those girls start talking trash,
a guy's got no defense.

Fig. 3

So hear me now, my brothers,
and remember what I say:
if a moon-eyed girl sits next to you,

GET UP AND **RUN AWAY!!**

Name: _____

They're Related

Directions: The bold word in each sentence below is derived from another word you likely already know. Use the meaning of the word you know to figure out what the bold word probably means in the sentence.

1. The firefighters had to wear extra **protection** on their faces.

   If *protect* means "keep something safe," then in this sentence, *protection* probably means _____

2. The children admitted to breaking the window; their action was not **defensible**.

   If *defense* means "excuse or reason for," then in this sentence, *defensible* probably means _____

3. Despite their **innocence**, many animals lost their homes in the forest fire.

   If *innocent* means "not guilty," then in this sentence, *innocence* probably means

   _____

4. No dogs were allowed, with the **exception** of seeing-eye dogs for the blind.

   If *except* means "not including," then in this sentence, *exception* probably means

   _____

5. The city put up a statue in **remembrance** of their beloved founder.

   If *remember* means "hold in memory," then in this sentence, *remembrance* probably means _____

6. Emissions from cars are a major **offender** in air pollution.

   If *offend* means "cause hurt or harm," then in this sentence, *offender* probably means _____

Name:_____

Sisters and Brothers

Directions: Find and circle the misspelled word in each sentence. Then write it correctly on the line.

_____   1. Shanell thought she was the girl of Devin's dreams, but than he broke her heart.

_____   2. Shanell proclaims, "So here me, all my sisters, and remember what I say…"

_____   3. "…protect yourselfs from lying boys like low down Devin Shay."

_____   4. Poor Devin. He's never had a girlfriend in his hole life…

_____   5. …not Shanell or anybudy else!

_____   6. The only thing he did was be nice to Shanell in the cafateria.

_____   7. He wouldn't have even cared what she rote about him…

_____   8. …accept now, every girl in school thinks he's a rat.

_____   9. He is totally innocent but with no defence!

_____   10. The only thing he had left to do was to warn the others: "if a moon-eyed girl sits necks to you, GET UP AND RUN AWAY!"

Extension

Pretend for a moment that you are Shanell. Write a paragraph (or poem) in response to Devin's poem.

Girl Monsters from Outer Space

In his next poem, sixth-grader Devin wants to be friends with girls but is confounded by their behavior. Unable to understand them or even communicate, he compares them to aliens.

Making Connections

- Help students connect their own experiences to what they are about to read. Ask, by a show of hands, who has ever felt that someone has gotten mad at them "for no reason." Of those who raised their hands, invite a few volunteers to share their experiences.

- Ask for another show of hands of those who agree with this statement: People don't get mad for no reason; there is always a reason. Allow students time to discuss and debate the statement.

- Tell students that they will listen to a poem in which Devin is upset because Sonia got mad at him "for no reason." Have students listen as you read the poem aloud. Afterward, ask whether anyone has changed his or her mind about the possibility of someone being mad "for no reason" and why.

Comprehension Strategy: 5 Ws

- Distribute copies of the poem or display it for the class.

- Explain that good readers check their understanding of what they read by asking questions. One of the easiest ways to do this is with the 5 Ws—*who/m*, *what*, *where*, *when*, and *why*. Practice with these: Whom is the poem about? What does Sonia want? Where does this exchange take place? When and why does Sonia get mad? After answering these, tell students that adding an *H* for *How* to the 5 W questions helps them understand even more. How does Devin react to Sonia's anger?

Standards-Based Skill Focus: Fluency—Prosody

- Tell students that *prosody* is the part of fluency in which readers use appropriate phrasing, tone, volume, and emphasis. Introduce this to students by comparing reading to singing. Demonstrate how one's voice drops down slightly at the end of a statement (declarative sentence) and goes up at the end of a question (interrogative sentence).

- Write these two sentences on the board and have students practice reading them aloud: I don't know what I think. What do you think?

- Use the same sentences to demonstrate how emphasizing different words colors the meaning. Examples: **What** do you think? What **do** you think? What do **you** think? Let students practice reading parts of Devin's poem with prosody.

- Reinforce this concept with the activity on page 56. Distribute copies of the page and have students complete it individually.

Vocabulary Word Study

- Distribute copies of page 57.

- Reinforce vocabulary used in the poem by challenging students to complete the puzzle. Before students begin, make sure they have a copy of the poem or can refer to it on display.

GIRL MONSTERS FROM OUTER SPACE

by Devin Shay

Girl Home Planet

Me   Sonia

2 seconds later

Me   Sonia

EARTH

Sonia sat next to me on the bus.
   "Devin," she said.
   "I've been thinking about cutting my hair short.
   What do you think?"

And I heard this voice in my head:
   I don't know what I think.
   What does she think?
   What if I don't think what she thinks?

And before I can get a word out,
Sonia stomps her foot,
tells me how clueless I am,
and moves to another seat.

I have no idea how it happens,
but it's like trying to talk to an alien.
What language does it speak?
What does it want me to do?
And if I make this creature angry,
will it slice me right in two?

Theoretically, I like girls—
from a distance they're sublime—
but when a girl gets close to me,
I lose it every time.

Name: _____

Sentence Tunes

Directions: Answer the questions below to test your ability to recognize sentence prosody—where to raise or drop your voice, or make it louder or softer.

1. Sonia said, "I've been thinking about cutting my hair short. What do you think?"

   a. What happens to your voice when you reach the period after the word *short*?

   _____

   b. What happens to your voice when you reach the question mark after the word *think*?

   _____

   c. In the question "What do you think?" which word should be emphasized (said a bit louder than the others)?

   _____

2. Devin thought: I don't know what I think. What if I don't think what she thinks?

   a. What happens to your voice when you reach the period after the word *think*?

   _____

   b. What happens to your voice when you reach the question mark after the word *thinks*?

   _____

   c. The question below is written with different words emphasized. As you read each one, say the underlined words a bit louder than the rest.

      1. What if <u>I</u> don't think what she thinks?

      2. What if I <u>don't</u> think what she thinks?

      3. What if I don't think what <u>she</u> thinks?

      4. What if I don't think what she <u>thinks</u>?

      Write the number of the sentence that best shows how it should be read. _____

Name: _____

Girl Monsters from Outer Space

Directions: Each answer in the word puzzle below can be found in Devin's poem "Girl Monsters from Outer Space." Use the clues given to identify the mystery word. Then write the word in the blanks inside the box below.

1. I heard this _____ in my head.

2. It's like trying to talk to an _____.

3. What _____ does it speak?

4. _____, I like girls.

5. From a distance they're _____.

6. If I make this _____ angry,

7. will it _____ me right in two?

8. Sonia _____ her foot.

1. __ __ __ __ ★ __ __ __
2. __ __ ★ __ __ __ __
3. __ __ __ __ __ ★ __ __ __ __ __
4. __ __ __ __ __ ★ __ __ __ __ __ __ __
5. __ __ __ __ ★ __ __ __
6. __ __ __ ★ __ __ __ __ __
7. __ ★ __ __ __ __
8. __ __ __ __ __ __ ★ __

When Devin didn't answer Sonia right away, what word did she use to describe him? To get the answer, write the word formed by the letters in the column under the star in the puzzle.

Mystery Word * ___ ___ ___ ___ ___ ___ ___ ___

Extension

After you figure out the mystery word, write two sentences that tell if you think it was an accurate description, and why or why not.

Between the Lines

In his next contribution in the collection of poems by the slam poetry team, Devin still can't understand girls but—at last—he finds one he can communicate with.

Making Connections

- Help students connect their own experiences to what they are about to read. Ask students to think of a time when someone said one thing but meant something else. Explain that sometimes people don't want to or can't express their true feelings, and the words they say do not match what they are actually feeling. Give an example such as this: A small child might say, "I hate you!" when he means that he is angry. Invite volunteers to share their thoughts or experiences about this.

- Tell students that they will listen to Devin's poem about Veronica. Ask them to listen for how Devin figures out Veronica's true feelings even though they are quite different from her actual words. Have students listen as you read the poem aloud.

Comprehension Strategy: Sequence

- Distribute copies of the poem or display it for the class.

- Explain to students that one strategy for reviewing what they read and checking their understanding is to sequence the main events or points using the words *First*, *Next*, *Then*, and *Finally* as a guide.

- Review the sequence of events in the poem by having students complete statements for each of the sequence words. Afterward, remind them that they can use this technique on their own to review what they read.

Standards-Based Skill Focus: Author's Device—Exaggeration

- Tell the class a claim that includes a clear exaggeration. For example, you could say, "Once I ran so fast that the rubber on my shoes began to smoke." Ask students to respond to your statement. Someone will say that it is unbelievable. Discuss why.

- Introduce the concept of *exaggeration*. Define it as overstatement or stretching the truth until it becomes an impossible claim.

- Ask students to find two examples of exaggeration in the poem (*only girl in the universe, never in a million years*). Explain that Devin uses these exaggerations to make his point about the uniqueness of Veronica's lipstick and the unlikelihood she would tell him to have a nice day.

- Have students complete the skill activity on individual copies of page 60.

Vocabulary Word Study

- Tell students that one of the main visual images in Devin's poem is Veronica's Vampire-Purple lipstick. Color words are good descriptors. Extend your students' color word vocabulary with the activity on page 61, which introduces them to color words beyond the basics.

- Distribute copies of page 61. Review the directions and then have students complete the page individually.

Between the Lines

by Devin Shay

There it was,
jagged lines of purple lipstick
slashed across a sheet of loose-leaf paper
taped to the door of my locker—

And the second I saw it,
I knew it was Veronica Page.
I knew because of the color of the lipstick—
Vampire Purple!
It's unmistakable,
and Veronica's the only girl in the universe who wears it.

I also knew why she did it.
It was her way of trying to be sweet,
but did she write, Have a nice day, Devin?
Never in a million years!
Remember,
we're talking about Vampire-Purple-Veronica-Page
and, for her, this was almost a love note.
So the next time I saw her I smiled and said,
"Thanks for the little note,"
to which she replied, "I knew you'd like it."

When it comes to understanding girls,
it's hard to read the signs,
but lately I've been learning
how to read between the lines.

Name:_____

That's an Exaggeration

Directions: Rewrite each statement below as an exaggeration. Don't worry about it being believable—exaggerations stretch the truth until they are impossible claims.

1. Once I ran very fast.

I ran so fast that _____.

2. He ate a lot at the party.

He ate so much that _____.

3. My sister talks too much on the phone.

She talks so much that _____.

4. It was a hot summer day.

It was so hot that _____.

5. The thunder was loud.

It was so loud that _____.

6. Mom said that my room was messy.

It was so messy that_____.

7. It was cold at the bus stop.

It was so cold that _____.

Name:_____

Between the Lines

Directions: Devin described Veronica's lipstick as "Vampire Purple." Color words are good to use in descriptions, but there are more than the eight basic colors. Use this activity to see if you can match more subtle color names to their descriptions. Afterward, compare answers with a friend and, if needed, check a dictionary.

Color	Description
1. scarlet	light or sky blue
2. azure	tan or light brown
3. chartreuse	intense red
4. khaki	yellow-green
5. indigo	reddish purple
6. magenta	deep blue-violet
7. russet	blue-green
8. turquoise	brownish gray
9. taupe	reddish brown
10. fuchsia	deep purplish pink

Extension

For each color above, think of something that you could describe with that color. For example: scarlet—lava flowing from a volcano.

Remote Control

In "Remote Control," Devin speculates about what it would be like to have a remote control that works on people.

• •

Making Connections

- Help students connect their own experiences to what they are about to read. Ask students to name everything they know that has a remote control. Make a list on the board.

- Ask students what it would be like to control another person with a remote control. What kinds of buttons would students like to have on the remote control? Give students time to discuss their ideas in pairs.

- Tell students that they will listen to a poem in which Devin uses a remote control on people. Have students listen as you read the poem aloud.

Comprehension Strategy: Author's Purpose

- Distribute copies of the poem or display it for the class.

- Remind students that authors write for different purposes, such as to inform, entertain, or persuade. Ask students what they think Devin's intended purpose was for writing this poem. If no one suggests it, pose the question "Could what happened in the poem happen in real life?"

Standards-Based Skill Focus: Sequence and Retell

- Tell students that one way to better understand and remember what has been read is to be able to retell what happened in the *beginning*, *middle*, and *end*.

- Distribute copies of page 64 to students. Tell students they are going to reread the poem and identify the main events that happen in the beginning, middle, and end of the poem. Have students identify these elements and write a one-sentence summary for each event. Then have students reread their sentences to see if they retell the events of the poem.

Vocabulary Word Study

- Write the words *math*, *science*, *reading*, and *social studies* on the board. Ask students what these words have in common. Ask students to think of one word that describes all these words. Tell students that since these words have something in common, we can give the group a name or category (*subjects*).

- Provide students practice identifying categories using words from the poem with the activity on page 65. Distribute the activity sheet and review the directions. The first word in each list of words is from the poem. Have students locate the words in the poem. Then have students complete the activity in pairs or individually.

REMOTE CONTROL

by Devin Shay

It's the best invention ever—
so powerful, so bold.
It fills my life with happiness—
the Human Remote Control!

My teacher was dangerously angry,
his fury absolute,
but when he tried to yell at us,
I put his mouth on mute.

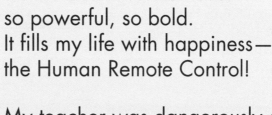

The principal came running.
She said, "Give me that device!"
But just in time I pressed the pause
and turned her into ice.

It's been a perfect day at school,
the best I ever had.
So now I think I'll take it home,
and try it on my dad.

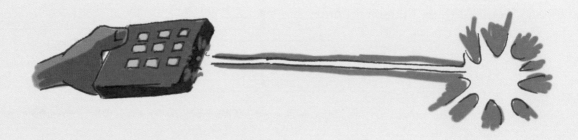

Name: _____

In My Own Words

Directions: Reread the poem below. Identify the main events in the poem. Write a one-sentence summary for each: the beginning, middle, and end.

It's the best invention ever—
so powerful, so bold.
It fills my life with happiness—
the Human Remote Control!

My teacher was dangerously angry,
his fury absolute,
but when he tried to yell at us,
I put his mouth on mute.

The principal came running.
She said, "Give me that device!"
But just in time I pressed the pause
and turned her into ice.

It's been a perfect day at school,
the best I ever had.
So now I think I'll take it home,
and try it on my dad.

Beginning

_____

_____

_____

Middle

_____

_____

_____

End

_____

_____

_____

Name:_____

Remote Control

Directions: Read each group of words. Decide what the words have in common. Write a name for the category.

Words	Category
1. happiness bliss joy	
2. yell whisper shout	
3. mouth eyes nose	
4. running walking jogging	
5. home nest cave	
6. dad mom sister	
7. angry surprised excited	
8. teacher doctor engineer	
9. powerful forceful strong	
10. bold brave fearless	

Extension

Choose another word from the poem. Think of a category title.
Then think of two other words that match the category.

Alvin "Nerd-One" Lofton

In the introduction about Alvin, we find out exactly why he is a nerd, not a geek.

Making Connections

- Help students connect their own experiences to what they are about to read. Ask students to describe a *nerd*. Allow students to discuss the word in pairs or small groups and then share their discussions with the whole class. Ask students if their responses are based on personal experiences with knowing someone who is a nerd or if they are based on the stereotypical description of a nerd.

- Have students describe a *geek*. What makes someone a geek? How is a geek different from a nerd?

- Tell students that they will listen to Shaneka's introduction about Alvin "Nerd-One" Lofton. Ask students to listen to how Shaneka describes Alvin and how Alvin describes himself. Have students listen as you read the introduction aloud.

Comprehension Strategy: Listening for Details

- Prior to distributing copies of the introduction or displaying it for the class, check how well students listened. Ask the following questions: What happened to deeply hurt Alvin's feelings? What interests does Alvin have? How are Alvin's interests different from the interests other people may have?

Standards-Based Skill Focus: Details

- Tell students that identifying the main idea of a text is important; however, by identifying the details in a text, they can gain greater insight into what they have read.

- Distribute copies of the introduction or display it for the class. Have students refer to the text as they review and discuss the questions in the Comprehension Strategy section. Ask students how many questions they were able to answer based on hearing the introduction. Ask students if the number of questions increased after they were able to review the actual text for the introduction.

- Provide students with practice identifying important details in text. Distribute copies of page 68 for students to complete.

Vocabulary Word Study

- Provide students with copies of the introduction. Have them read the text and highlight any words they do not know. Tell students that having a good understanding of these words will help their comprehension.

- Distribute copies of page 69. Tell students that this page contains the definitions of some of the words from Shaneka's introduction to Alvin with which they may not be familiar. Have them use the code to find the word that matches each definition.

None of us are responsible for Alvin's nickname; he chose it himself. When we said we were reluctant to call him a nerd, he acted shocked and said he was "deeply wounded." But don't call him a geek. He'll go ballistic.

"According to Wikipedia," he explained, "a geek is a person who obsesses in one area or another, whereas a nerd is a highly intelligent person who is very scholarly and does well in many domains such as math, science, and computing. That's me," he said, "a nerd, not a geek." I'm still not sure I get the difference, but if Alvin says he's a nerd and not a geek, I'm sure he's got it right. Because that's what Alvin does: he gets it right. Alvin learns things, and not just school things. He learns anything and everything there is to know. It's what he does for fun.

Alvin's probably the smartest kid in the country. He's also one of the biggest, and he's unbelievably coordinated. In the beginning of sixth grade, we were at PE shooting hoops, and Alvin sunk four three-point shots in a row. "Dude," I said, "you could be a superstar."

"Shaneka," he said, "I'm already a superstar. I'm Nerd-One." Then he gave me the Vulcan salute. (He then went on to explain that the salute was a kind of ironic joke. "Nerds don't do Vulcan salutes," he said, very amused with himself. "That's a geek thing.")

So Alvin doesn't dream about being a professional athlete, but he does have a dream. He wants to win the Nobel Prize for Physics, and I'm bettin' he'll do it. Alvin knows all about the great scientists, not just what they discovered, but when and where they lived, and what they were like. He knows science like some guys know sports, and when he talks about it, he makes it interesting and easy to understand.

Alvin says that "science is like the air we breathe: it's real and it's everywhere and it's why things happen the way they do." So when Alvin stretches a rubber band he thinks: potential energy. Or when he sees a flash of lightning he thinks: balancing electrical charges. It blew him away when he discovered that other people don't think that way. That's when he named himself Nerd-One. "I suddenly realized that I really was a nerd," he says laughing. "Then I realized how cool it was to be a nerd and how boring it would be to be normal."

Name:_____

It's in the Details

Directions: You know Alvin is a nerd, but what else do you know? Review Shaneka's introduction of Alvin to find the answer to the questions below.

1. Why does Alvin say he is a nerd and not a geek? _____

_____

_____

2. How is Alvin's physical appearance described? _____

_____

3. What does Alvin do as an ironic joke? Why is it ironic?_____

_____

_____

4. What is Alvin's dream? _____

_____

5. What consumes Alvin's thoughts? Provide one specific example._____

_____

6. Why does Alvin think it is cool to be a nerd? _____

_____

7. Who gave Alvin the nickname "Nerd-One?"_____

_____

Name:_____

Alvin "Nerd-One" Lofton

Directions: Read the definitions below. Use the code to make the words that are being defined.

Code

a = 12	f = 19	k = 23	p = 15	u = 10
b = 5	g = 6	l = 7	q = 24	v = 25
c = 8	h = 21	m = 13	r = 2	w = 14
d = 4	i = 3	n = 9	s = 16	x = 11
e = 1	j = 22	o = 18	t = 17	y = 20

1. to move together

___ ___ ___ ___ ___ ___ ___ ___ ___ ___ ___
8   18   18   2   4   3   9   12   17   1   4

2. characteristic of a learned person

___ ___ ___ ___ ___ ___ ___ ___ ___
16   8   21   18   7   12   2   7   20

3. occupies the mind

___ ___ ___ ___ ___ ___ ___ ___
18   5   16   1   16   16   1   16

4. hesitant

___ ___ ___ ___ ___ ___ ___ ___ ___
2   1   7   10   8   17   12   9   17

5. incongruity

___ ___ ___ ___ ___ ___
3   2   18   9   3   8

6. possibility

___ ___ ___ ___ ___ ___ ___ ___ ___
15   18   17   1   9   17   3   12   7

7. science that deals with energy

___ ___ ___ ___ ___ ___ ___
15   21   20   16   3   8   16

8. hard to believe

___ ___ ___ ___ ___ ___ ___ ___ ___ ___ ___ ___
10   9   5   1   7   3   1   25   12   5   7   20

Extension

Look back at the text. Highlight each of the words you decoded above. Reread the sentence the word is in. Do you understand the sentence better now?

Crystal Cool

In his first poem, we quickly find out that Alvin has a talent for combining entertaining poetry with curriculum content. Here he tells us about rocks, but in a cool way.

Making Connections

- Help students connect their own experiences to what they are about to read.

- Write on the board the terms *sedimentary*, *metamorphic*, and *igneous*. Provide some background on the terms. *Sedimentary rock* comes from sediment, which is material that settles to the bottom. *Metamorphic* rock is formed when sedimentary rock changes. Point out that the term *morph* means *to change*. The term *igneous* comes from an old Latin word, *ignis*, meaning "fire". It is also the origin of the word *ignite*, meaning "catch on fire." Igneous rock is formed when a fiery volcano erupts. The molten lava cools and hardens into igneous rock.

- Tell students that they will listen to a poem in which Alvin talks about the different kinds of rocks. Have students listen as you read the poem aloud.

Comprehension Strategy: Author's Purpose— Inform/Entertain

- Distribute copies of the poem or display it for the class.

- Remind students that authors write for different purposes, such as to inform, entertain, or persuade. Ask students what they think Alvin's intended purpose was for writing this poem. If no one suggests it, pose the question "Could he have had two purposes—to both inform and entertain?"

Standards-Based Skill Focus: Transitions

- Have students find and circle these words in the poem: Stanza 1—*and*, Stanza 2—*now*, Stanza 3—*which*, Stanza 4—*then*, Stanza 5—*when*, and Stanza 6—*but*.

- Have a student read aloud the entire stanza in which the target word appears. Ask a student to read what comes just before the target word and then what comes after it. Point out that the target word is used to connect ideas or to transition from one idea to another.

- Explain that *transition words* help text flow smoothly by directing readers to move from one idea to the next.

- The activity on page 72 offers practice with identifying transitions. Distribute copies of the activity sheet for students to complete individually or in pairs.

Vocabulary Word Study

- Have students find and highlight the following words in the poem: *sedimentary*, *metamorphic*, *igneous*, *moistens*, *morphing*, *molten*, *thermal*, and *molecules*. Have students reread the portion of text in which each word appears. If necessary, clarify for students the meaning of the word as it is used.

- Distribute copies of page 73, which checks students' understanding of these terms. You may choose to do the page together as a group, or ask students to complete it individually.

CRYSTAL COOL

by Alvin Lofton

METAMORPHIC

SEDIMENTARY

IGNEOUS

I've put three different kinds of rock
each in a separate jar,
and clearly labeled each of them
to tell us what they are.

Sedimentary. Metamorphic. Igneous.
And now I'll help you see
exactly what each rock is like
and how it came to be.

Sedimentary rocks are formed underwater
with layers of settling crud,
which is why when someone moistens them,
they smell a lot like mud.

Then with some heat and pressure,
the morphing soon appears.
Sedimentary becomes metamorphic,
in about ten thousand years.

And when molten magma comes out of the Earth,
it endures a thermal shock—
it hits the air, the molecules cool,
it turns into an igneous rock.

Which is why an IGNEOUS rock and I
are each a remarkable jewel.
We were once too hot to handle,
but now we're totally cool.

Name:_____

Transitions

Directions: Transitions are words or phrases used to connect ideas or to move the reader from one idea to the next. First, study the examples below. Then, for each passage, find and circle the transition word.

Examples: Look at the label on each jar (and) read how each rock was formed.
You have seen the different rocks. (Now) can you tell the difference?
They may look similar, (but) they were formed by very different processes.

1. Alvin put three different kinds of rocks each in a separate jar, and clearly labeled them.

2. The three kinds are sedimentary, metamorphic, and igneous. Now you will learn how they came to be.

3. Sedimentary rocks are formed underwater when sediment settles on the bottom, which is why if you get a dry sedimentary rock wet, it can smell like mud.

4. Ten thousand years go by. Heat and pressure condense the sediment. Then, the compressed rock has morphed, or changed, into a harder form—metamorphic.

5. Sedimentary and metamorphic rocks are related, but igneous comes from somewhere else.

6. You may know that rock on the surface of the Earth is hard and solid. However, deep under the surface, the temperature is so high that the rock is molten, or melted into a liquid.

7. The molten rock, or magma, is usually trapped way underground, which is why we don't notice it.

8. However, we certainly notice it when it finds its way out through a volcano!

9. Igneous rock is formed when molten magma finds its way to the surface. The magma begins to cool immediately and hardens. After cooling completely, the result is igneous rock.

Name:_____

Crystal Cool

Directions: Check your understanding of words from the poem "Crystal Cool." Answer the questions below. Use the poem or a dictionary if you need help.

1. When sedimentary rocks are moistened, they can smell a bit like mud. Would something *moistened* be dry, stinky, or wet? _____

2. Heat and pressure cause *morphing* of rock. Is the rock softening or changing?

   _____

3. Is *igneous* rock formed by heating or cooling of magma? _____

4. Which word best describes *molecules*: tiny, hot, or granular? _____

5. Which of these words does not fit with the others: *thermos*, *thermal*, *theory*, *thermometer*? _____ Why? _____

   _____

6. Where would you be likely to find *sedimentary rock*: near a volcano, on an island, or in a dry lake bed? _____

7. Is rock that is *molten* in the form of a solid, liquid, or gas? _____

Extension

Alvin's poem was both informative and entertaining. Which part did you like better—learning about rocks or being entertained by Alvin? Write your choice. Then write two more sentences—one stating something you learned about rocks and the other stating something you learned about Alvin.

Knowing the Why

In his second poem, Alvin muses about math—not so much the *what* as the *why*.

Making Connections

- Help students connect their own experiences to what they are about to read. Ask students to think about how they feel about the various subjects they study at school, such as language, math, and science. Ask them to choose which subject they enjoy most and least and why. After giving students time to reflect, ask a few volunteers to share their thoughts.

- Tell students that they will listen to a poem in which Alvin expresses his frustration with math—not because he dislikes it or has trouble doing it but for a different reason. Have students listen as you read the poem aloud. Afterward, ask someone to tell about Alvin's frustration with math.

Comprehension Strategy: Phrasing for Fluency

- Distribute copies of the poem or display it for the class.

- Write the following line on the board with no punctuation: *Alvin knows the rule and how to apply it but doesn't understand why*. Read the sentence.

- Ask a student to come to the board and draw a slash mark (/) between words to break the sentence into phrases. (Alvin knows the rule / and how to apply it / but doesn't understand why.) Read it again with these breaks.

- Explain to students that breaking sentences into phrases sounds more natural and makes reading easier to understand. Have students practice reading the poem in phrases.

Standards-Based Skill Focus: Double Negatives

- Write the following sentence on the board and ask students what, if anything, is wrong with it: *Don't never forget your math homework*.

- Underline the words *Don't never*. Point out that *don't* means *do not* and is a negative. The word *never* means *not ever* and is also a negative.

- Explain that in math, you may have two negatives, but in language, there should never be two negatives in the same sentence. One way to remember this is that the word *never* shouldn't be in the same sentence with any of the *not* contractions, such as *isn't, doesn't, wasn't, can't, don't*, etc.

- Distribute copies of page 76. Review the directions and then either do the activity together as a group or have students do it individually and then correct it as a group.

Vocabulary Word Study

- Tell students that classifying words is an excellent way to reinforce or check word knowledge.

- Distribute copies of page 77. Read the word list together. Then direct students to classify the words into the given categories. If necessary, allow students to work in pairs or small groups for support.

Knowing the WHY
by Alvin Lofton

Don't get me wrong,
I knew the rule and I knew how to apply it:
a negative times a negative makes a positive.
$-2 \times -2 = +4$
I knew the rule backwards and forwards,
but I didn't understand why.
Why does a negative times another negative make a positive?

I read books in the library.
I Googled it.
I even talked to a college professor,
and now I understand.

It's the kind of thing I like to do—
you might want to give it a try.
Knowing the **what** is a meaningless bore.
The cool part is knowing the **why**.

Name:_____

Never, Ever

Directions: Rewrite each sentence so that it does not contain a double negative.

> **Example:** Alvin doesn't never forget his math homework.
> 1. Alvin never forgets his homework.
> 2. Alvin doesn't ever forget his homework.

1. Mom says that I don't never eat enough vegetables.

   _____

2. Trevor wasn't never more surprised.

   _____

3. My sister doesn't never seem to get off the phone.

   _____

4. I try, but I can't never remember all those rules.

   _____

5. I am late sometimes, but it isn't never more than a few minutes.

   _____

NEGATIVE x NEGATIVE = POSITIVE

Name: _____

Knowing the Why

Directions: Alvin's poem "Knowing the Why" is about *mathematics*, which you know is the study of relationships using numbers. Below are two other categories of things you learn about—*geography*: the study of the Earth's features and *astronomy*: the study of space and the universe. The word list contains terms that are mostly associated with one of these study topics. Your job is to classify the words. Write each under the category in which it fits best.

percent	climate	satellite	numeral
island	meteor	glacier	equation
asteroid	orbit	solar	arctic
telescope	decimal	compass	symmetry
landform	square	globe	fraction
erosion	lunar	integer	comet
eclipse	equator	angle	

Mathematics Words	Geography Words	Astronomy Words

Extension

If you had to choose a career you would like in the future, what would it be? What subjects would you have to learn extensively or apply to do your job? For example, a weather forecaster would have to know geography; a real estate agent would need to understand math.

Brain Power

In Alvin's next poem, he is concerned about energy and suggests using brain power to find alternative energy sources.

Making Connections

- Help students connect their own experiences to what they are about to read. Ask students to think of three ways they used energy in the last 24 hours. If necessary, prompt them with the following questions: Did you use any hot water? Did you ride in a car? Did you use a computer? Did you watch TV? Ask students where they think the energy came from to heat water, fuel a car, or provide electricity.

- Ask students if they think conservation is important and why. Finally, ask a few volunteers to explain what it means to "go green."

- Tell students that they will listen to a poem in which Alvin tells about the different ways we can get energy and why we need more renewable energy sources. Have students listen as you read the poem aloud.

Comprehension Strategy: Previewing Text

- Distribute copies of the poem or display it for the class.

- Explain that a good way to approach text that may have technical or unfamiliar terms is to preview the text. Ask students to skim the poem to find and highlight such terms. Write these on the board and discuss their meanings. Examples: CO_2 (the symbol for carbon dioxide), *atomic fusion* (a nuclear reaction that releases energy), *geothermal* (heat contained inside Earth).

Standards-Based Skill Focus: Using Reference Materials

- Tell students that using reference materials used to mean having to look through a book such as a dictionary or encyclopedia. Although these are still valid, today's students also have the opportunity to use the Internet.

- Make only one copy of page 80. Cut apart the environment-related terms and give out one word per student or two per pair of students to research and report back to the class on the findings. Note that some terms can have applications for other topics. As you distribute the words, direct students to find the meanings that are relevant to energy, conservation, or the environment.

Vocabulary Word Study

- Distribute copies of page 81.

- Be sure that you have reviewed the words from page 80 and their meanings before having students complete this activity. Ideally, have the students who received these as their research words explain their meanings. Clarify and expound on their explanations as needed.

Brain Power

by Alvin Lofton

The facts are in, it's really true,
we're making too much CO_2.
So energy from fossil fuel
is fast becoming so uncool.

If Earth is where we want to stay,
we've got to find another way.
And we can do it if we're smart;
great minds have given us a start.

Atomic fusion from the sun
makes solar power number one.

A windmill spun by moving air
gets energy from everywhere.

And geothermal's all around.
It's steamy water underground.

And conservation? Can you guess?
Makes energy by using…LESS!

So don't go hide beneath your bed;
just use that thing inside your head.
To counteract the power drain,
use the power of your brain.

WIND

SOLAR

CONSERVE

Geothermal

#50240—The Poet and the Professor: Poems for Building Reading Skills

Name: _____

Research and Report

Directions: Find the meaning of each term as it relates to energy, conservation, or the environment. Be prepared to share your findings with the class.

consume	energy	fossil fuel
ozone	habitat	global
extinct	carbon	species
erosion	contaminate	landfill
pesticide	pollution	geothermal
conservation	endangered	population
recycle	catastrophe	diminish
emission	radioactive	fumes
resources	renewable	biosphere
atomic fusion	ecosystem	contaminant

Name: _____

Brain Power

Directions: Check your understanding of these words related to energy and the environment. Use words from the box below to fill in the missing words in the sentences.

consume	fusion	carbon	species	conservation
fossil	global	recycle	renewable	

1. CO_2 is the symbol for _____ dioxide.

2. Solar power comes from atomic _____ from the sun.

3. Saving energy by using less is one form of _____.

4. Coal and gas are types of _____ fuels.

5. The overuse of resources is a worldwide, or a _____ problem.

6. We need to find and use more _____ sources of energy.

7. Everyone can help by cutting down on waste and _____ when possible.

8. If everyone would _____ a little less, it would make a difference.

9. We owe to ourselves and every other _____ that share our planet to protect Earth's future.

Extension

Alvin's poem was about using renewable forms of energy rather than fossil fuels. What do you think is the best approach to ensure that we have the power we need today and also in the future? Write a paragraph that states your position and that tries to convince the reader to agree with you.

Protein Passion

In his next poem, Alvin writes about an experience he had with "flirting" with a girl.

Making Connections

- Help students connect their own experiences to what they are about to read. Ask students what it means to *flirt*. What does it look like? What does it sound like? Allow students time to reflect and then to share their ideas or their experiences.

- Tell students that they will listen to a poem in which Alvin tells about a girl who thought he was flirting with her, and how although he was not, the experience left him interested in her. Have students listen as you read the poem aloud.

Comprehension Strategy: Author's Purpose

- Distribute copies of the poem or display it for the class.

- Tell students that authors write for different purposes. Ask students to reread the poem with the intent to identify the author's purpose. Give students time to discuss their ideas with each other and then have them share their ideas with the class.

- Ask students if it is possible for the author to have two purposes: to entertain and to inform. Have students discuss this idea and come to a conclusion about the author's purpose of this poem.

Standards-Based Skill Focus: Synonyms

- Ask students what *synonyms* are. After defining it as words that mean the same or almost the same, tell students that identifying synonyms is an excellent way to extend their vocabularies.

- Distribute copies of page 84. Then complete the page together as a group. Have a different student read aloud each word and the accompanying word choices. Then have every student choose the word he or she thinks does not belong with the others.

- After completing the page, ask various students to reveal their choices and explain why their choices did not belong with the others.

Vocabulary Word Study

- Tell students that acquiring a rich vocabulary involves more than just learning words used in everyday speech and writing. Tell students that the poem contains many words with which they may be unfamiliar, including some content words.

- Distribute copies of page 85, which contains vocabulary words from the poem. You may wish to have students locate the words in the poem. After introducing and discussing each term, let students find each term in the word search.

PROTEIN PASSION

by Alvin Lofton

She said it to my face.
"Alvin," she said.
"Stop flirting with me."
And I was flabbergasted.

First of all,
I was not flirting with her.
I was being nice to her.
She's new at our school,
she was sitting on a bench by herself,
and she looked lonely.
I spend most of my life being lonely,
so I know how it feels,
and I thought a little conversation might help.

So I sat down beside her,
picked up a leaf,
and said the first thing that popped in my head.
"Roshanda," I began, "this leaf is capable of photosynthesis
because it contains a remarkable protein that scientists call…."

"Alvin," she said, interrupting my explanation.
"I know all about RuBisCO.
It's probably the most abundant protein on Earth.
It's important for its ability to catalyze the chemical reaction
by which inorganic carbon enters the biosphere,
and if we ever engineer a more efficient version,
we'll have the power to feed the world."
Which is when she told me to stop flirting with her
and walked away.

I thought I was the only seventh grader in the world
who knew anything about RuBisCO;
and now I discover there's another.
Her name is Roshanda.
We go to the same school,
and she assumes a conversation about catalytic protein is flirtatious.

Okay Roshanda, have it your way,
for now I'm just a friend.
But I promise you this, in a few more years,
we'll be talking RuBisCO again.

Name:_____

Means the Same

Directions: Read the first word in each line. Then read the word choices. Circle the word that does not belong with the rest. Be prepared to explain your choices.

1. explanation	account	answer	beneath
2. capable	able	adept	miniature
3. nice	pleasant	seldom	friendly
4. abundant	starve	ample	abounding
5. lonely	alone	secluded	hinder
6. interrupt	break in	disturb	accumulate
7. spend	invest	bestow	respond
8. conversation	chat	portion	comment
9. power	capability	seize	capacity
10. flirt	banter	tease	remark
11. remarkable	hold	outstanding	distinguished
12. important	chief	display	vital

Name:_____

Protein Passion

Directions: First, be sure that you can read each word in the box below and know what it means. If necessary, use a dictionary to look up each word. Then find each word in the word search. Look up, down, and diagonally.

photosynthesis	flabbergasted	catalytic	remarkable	protein
efficient	biosphere	abundant	inorganic	carbon

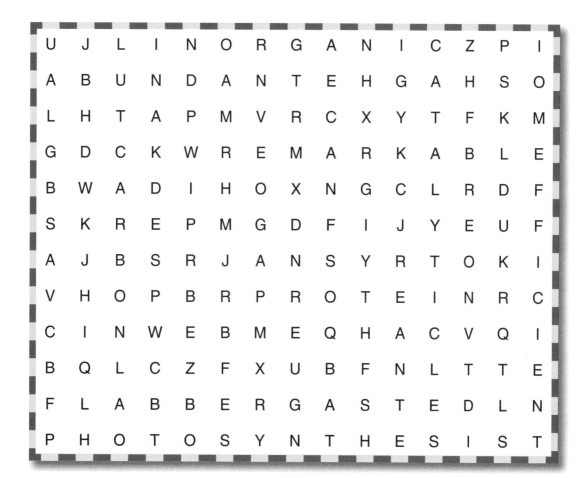

```
U  J  L  I  N  O  R  G  A  N  I  C  Z  P  I
A  B  U  N  D  A  N  T  E  H  G  A  H  S  O
L  H  T  A  P  M  V  R  C  X  Y  T  F  K  M
G  D  C  K  W  R  E  M  A  R  K  A  B  L  E
B  W  A  D  I  H  O  X  N  G  C  L  R  D  F
S  K  R  E  P  M  G  D  F  I  J  Y  E  U  F
A  J  B  S  R  J  A  N  S  Y  R  T  O  K  I
V  H  O  P  B  R  P  R  O  T  E  I  N  R  C
C  I  N  W  E  B  M  E  Q  H  A  C  V  Q  I
B  Q  L  C  Z  F  X  U  B  F  N  L  T  T  E
F  L  A  B  B  E  R  G  A  S  T  E  D  L  N
P  H  O  T  O  S  Y  N  T  H  E  S  I  S  T
```

Extension

Identify the science-related words above. Write a sentence using each word.

Stairway to the Stars

In his final poem, Alvin takes us up the stairs of the atmospheric layers that surround Earth.

Making Connections

- Help students connect their own experiences to what they are about to read. Ask who has ever looked in the sky and wondered how high it goes or where it ends. Give students time to reflect, and then invite a few volunteers to speculate on the answers to these questions.

- Tell students that they will listen to a poem in which Alvin tells us how high the sky goes and where it ends. Have students listen as you read the poem.

Comprehension Strategy: Recognizing Figurative Language

- Distribute copies of the poem or display it for the class.

- Have students find and highlight the following phrases in the poem: *layers, like giant atmospheric stairs* and *base become our stairway into space*. Explain that these are examples of *figurative language*—a way of describing something by comparing it to or representing it as something else. When the comparison uses the words *like* or *as*, it is called a *simile* (as in *layers, like giant atmospheric stairs*, which compares the layers of the atmosphere to a stairway). A direct comparison of one thing to another is called a *metaphor*, (as in *base become our stairway into space*, which directly compares the layers to a stairway). Remind students to keep looking for figurative language in their reading.

Standards-Based Skill Focus: Deconstructing Words for Meaning

- Tell students that *construct* means "to build," so *deconstruct* means "to tear down or take apart." Deconstructing words can be a good strategy for determining word meaning.

- Write the following terms on the board: *troposphere, stratosphere, mesosphere, thermosphere*, and *exosphere*. First, ask students what all of the words have in common. (They all contain *–sphere*.) Explain that because they know that *sphere* means *ball or round-shaped*, they know that all of these words describe something round-shaped, such as a layer around Earth.

- Distribute copies of page 88. Review the directions for finding the meanings of the words by deconstructing them. Then have students complete the activity independently.

Vocabulary Word Study

- Distribute copies of page 89.

- Reinforce students' vocabulary knowledge about the layers of the atmosphere. Have students complete the couplets. They can reference the poem as needed. Afterward, call on five students to read aloud the couplets.

STAIRWAY TO THE STARS

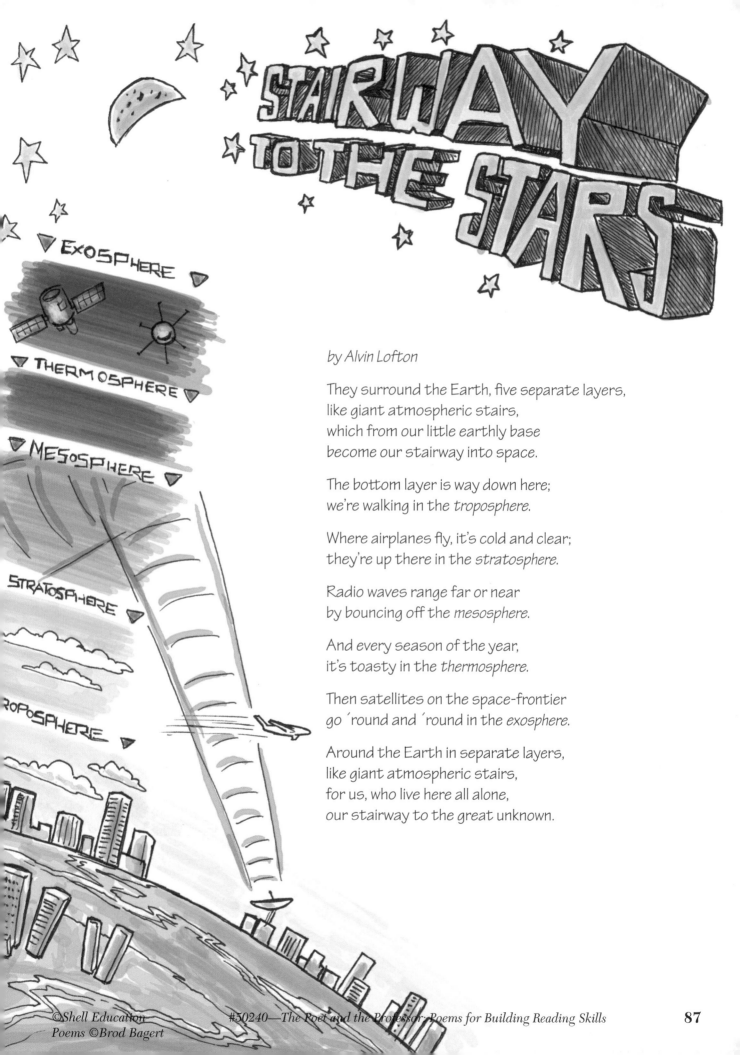

EXOSPHERE

THERMOSPHERE

MESOSPHERE

STRATOSPHERE

TROPOSPHERE

by Alvin Lofton

They surround the Earth, five separate layers,
like giant atmospheric stairs,
which from our little earthly base
become our stairway into space.

The bottom layer is way down here;
we're walking in the *troposphere*.

Where airplanes fly, it's cold and clear;
they're up there in the *stratosphere*.

Radio waves range far or near
by bouncing off the *mesosphere*.

And every season of the year,
it's toasty in the *thermosphere*.

Then satellites on the space-frontier
go 'round and 'round in the *exosphere*.

Around the Earth in separate layers,
like giant atmospheric stairs,
for us, who live here all alone,
our stairway to the great unknown.

Name:_____

Deconstructing Words

Directions: Study the meanings of the word parts in the box below. Use them to help you figure out which description matches each term. Draw a line to connect each vocabulary word to its definition.

tropo—turning, change	*strato*—layer	*meso*—middle
thermo—heat	*exo*—outer or outside	

1. troposphere

2. stratosphere

3. mesosphere

4. thermosphere

5. exosphere

Of the five layers of atmosphere, this falls in the middle, where the temperature falls rapidly. It is in this layer that we can see meteor showers.

This is the lowest layer of atmosphere—the one in which we live, where the air constantly turns and temperature and conditions are always changing.

This is a layer of atmosphere that runs from about 6–30 miles above Earth. Within this layer are several sub-layers, including the ozone layer.

Of the five layers of atmosphere, this is the outermost layer and extends to about 40,000 miles out from Earth's surface.

This atmospheric layer, which begins about 53 miles above Earth, is characterized by large fluctuations of temperature. Here, there are few molecules, so heat from the sun can be absorbed and lost easily.

Name:_____

Stairway to the Stars

Directions: Below is a diagram representing these layers of the atmosphere that blanket Earth. Complete each couplet by writing in the name of the layer.

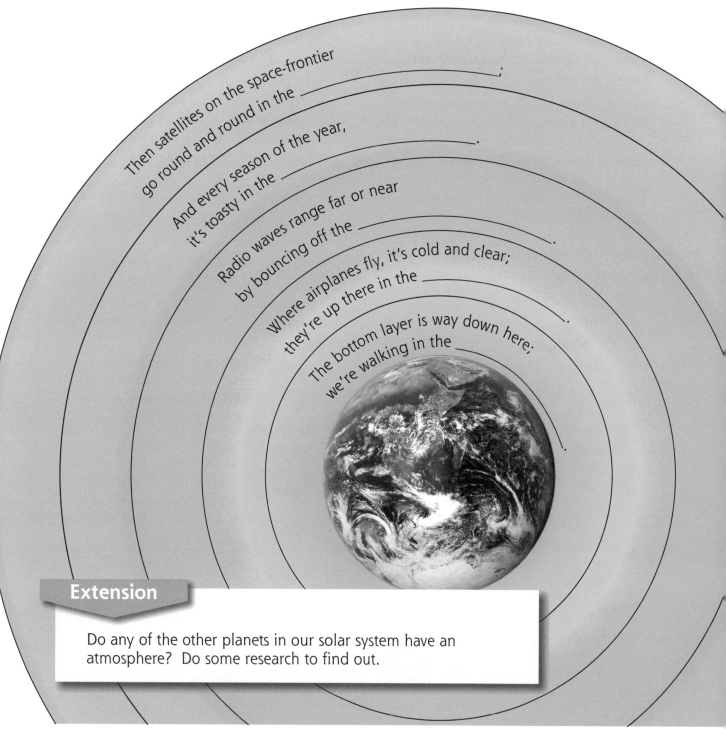

Then satellites on the space-frontier
go round and round in the _____;

And every season of the year,
it's toasty in the _____.

Radio waves range far or near
by bouncing off the _____.

Where airplanes fly, it's cold and clear;
they're up there in the _____.

The bottom layer is way down here;
we're walking in the _____.

Extension

Do any of the other planets in our solar system have an atmosphere? Do some research to find out.

Armando "El Fuego" Martí

The next person Shaneka introduces us to is Armando "El Fuego" Martí. Armando dislikes "the establishment" and wants to learn, not for tests, but for the sake of learning.

Making Connections

- Help students connect their own experiences to what they are about to read.

- Tell students that they are going to be listening to an introduction by Shaneka about another member of the poetry team—Armando "El Fuego" Martí. Ask students to listen for clues about the kind of person Armando is as you read aloud the introduction.

Comprehension Strategy: Questioning

- Tell students that sometimes not all questions can be answered by looking back at the text. It is the role of the reader to try to use what is known to answer the unknown. In the end, there are some questions that will remain unanswered.

- Distribute copies of the introduction or display it for the class. Challenge students to answer these critical thinking questions: Why does Armando feel so strongly about learning? What does the teacher say about Armando's poem? Why does Armando change the name of his poem? Why does Armando not stand up to the teacher when she talks to him about the poem? Why does Armando not like to talk about his family?

- Encourage students to seek the answers to some of the questions above, not only in the introduction but also as they read the poems by Armando.

Standards-Based Skill Focus: Capitalization—Proper Nouns

- Remind students that the names of people are always capitalized. The specific names of people are called *proper nouns*. Give examples such as: Alfred (a particular boy), Ms. McBride (a particular teacher), and South Korea (a particular country).

- Have students identify the proper nouns that are names in the introduction (Armando, Ms. McBride, and Pancho Villa).

- Distribute copies of page 92 for students to complete individually. Ask a volunteer to read the story aloud. Finally, ask students to identify the names they found.

Vocabulary Word Study

- Tell students that being able to read and write a word does not make it part of their vocabularies. They must also know and understand the word's meanings.

- Ask students to find and underline the following words in the introduction: *pounds, change, right, ground, rest, back,* and *case*. Explain that each of these words has more than one meaning.

- Distribute copies of page 93 and have students use context clues to determine which meaning applies in each sentence. Review their choices at the end of the activity.

Armando "El Fuego" Martí

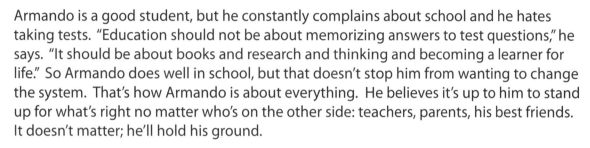

When you first meet Armando, you don't see much. He's the shortest kid in the class, and he weighs about two pounds, but that all changes the second you look at his eyes. He has these black hawk eyes that look inside you, like he knows all your secrets.

Armando is a good student, but he constantly complains about school and he hates taking tests. "Education should not be about memorizing answers to test questions," he says. "It should be about books and research and thinking and becoming a learner for life." So Armando does well in school, but that doesn't stop him from wanting to change the system. That's how Armando is about everything. He believes it's up to him to stand up for what's right no matter who's on the other side: teachers, parents, his best friends. It doesn't matter; he'll hold his ground.

And yes, sometimes Armando can be stubborn, but he's not a hardhead. Last November, right before Thanksgiving, Armando wrote a poem called "Test Zombies." It was about how bad our teachers were for doing nothing but giving us tests. When he read the poem in class, I remember thinking, this time Armando may have gone too far. We didn't have long to wait. That very afternoon Ms. McBride walked right up to Armando in the middle of slam poetry practice. "I want to talk to you about that poem," she said. Then she looked around at the rest of us and added, "Out in the hall." The two of them walked out. Five minutes later, Armando came back by himself, but he wouldn't tell us what happened. "I need to think about it," was all we could get out of him.

A week later, he changed the title of that poem to "The Flame" and rewrote it to say that it wasn't the teacher's fault. "Dude," I teased. "I hear you wimped out and changed your poem just because a teacher got on your case."

"It's not their fault," he said. "They didn't sign up to be testgivers, they signed up to be teachers. They give their lives to be our teachers, and most of them hate those stupid tests more than we do. I thought about it. I decided I was wrong and I changed the poem. If that's being a wimp, then I'm a wimp."

That's how it is for Armando—with a poem, with the educational system, with the problems of the world. If something's wrong, Armando thinks it's up to him to fix it. If you remind him that he's just 13, he'll tell you how his great-great-grandfather was younger than that when he fought for Pancho Villa in the Mexican Revolution. He's always telling people about that great-great-grandfather, but he never talks about the rest of his family, not even with his best friends. In fourth grade, we had to write a paragraph about our family, and Armando wrote about the stray cat he feeds in the alley behind his house. The cat's name? Pancho Villa.

Name: _____

Proper Names

Directions: You know that names of particular people should begin with capital letters. Sam forgot this as he wrote the story below. The proofreader's mark for capitalize is three lines (≡) drawn under the letter that needs to be capitalized. Draw three lines under any letter that should be capitalized in the story.

My name is sam hawkins. My best friend is dimitri rosen. He is a fun guy, but sometimes I think he is on another planet—like mars. Last week, we went to park mall to see a movie. While we were in line at the theater, dimitri suddenly got all dreamy-eyed.

"Look, sam," he whispered. "Look at the girl in the pink sweatshirt."

I looked. I was not impressed. In fact, I was grossed out. It was my sister beth. She and her friends were in line to see another movie. Before I could say anything, he started walking over toward them. I didn't want to lose our place in line. I just watched, but pretended I wasn't.

Of course, he didn't talk to beth first. He approached one of her friends—julie—and tapped her on the shoulder. He caught their attention all right. I could see beth, julie, and maria all look at dimitri with the evil-eye. It was beth who said something, and then they all laughed. dimitri looked down at the floor and slowly returned to our line.

I decided not to tell him that beth was my sister. Instead I just asked him how it went. Without looking up at me he said, "Up close, she wasn't all that."

They obviously made dimitri feel bad, so I tried to soften the blow. "Maybe beth just isn't your type," I said.

"beth?" dimitri said, and now looked me straight in the eye. "How do you know her name?"

Uh-oh. I thought. I'm busted. I had to confess. "Those three are practically in high school—julie marcos, maria beckham, and beth hawkins— that's hawkins, dude. beth hawkins is my sister. You went over there before I had the chance to tell you!"

Name:_____

Armando "El Fuego" Martí

Directions: Read each sentence. Decide which meaning of the bold word applies in that sentence. Write the number on the line.

_____ **1.** I hear you wimped out and changed your poem just because a teacher **got on your case**.

1) container for carrying
2) nagged at
3) an occurrence

_____ **2.** So Armando does well in school, but that doesn't stop him from wanting to **change** the system.

1) coins
2) to make different
3) to give or get smaller amounts of money

_____ **3.** He's the shortest kid in class, and he weighs about two **pounds**.

1) units of measurement
2) a place for stray dogs
3) hits

_____ **4.** Five minutes later, Armando **came back** by himself, but he wouldn't tell us what happened.

1) the rear
2) reversed
3) returned

_____ **5.** Then she looked around at the **rest** of us.

1) freedom from activity
2) the part that is left
3) sleep

_____ **6.** He believes it's up to him to stand up for what's right no matter who's on the other side: teachers, parents, his best friends. It doesn't matter; he'll **hold his ground**.

1) the solid surface of the Earth
2) maintain a position
3) the garden or lawn surrounding a building

_____ **7.** He believes it's up to him to stand up for what's **right**.

1) genuine
2) being in accordance with what is good
3) being in good mental health

Extension

Use each of the seven words/phrases in sentences of your own. In each sentence use the word/phrase with a meaning different from the ones used in the sentences on this page.

Teacher Police

Right from his first poem, we find out that Armando is all about justice, fairness, and making things the way he thinks they should be. His first topic of protest—parent-teacher night.

Making Connections

- Help students connect their own experiences to what they are about to read. Discuss the purpose of parent-teacher night. Then ask students to think about how they feel about it. Is it something they dread, is it something they look forward to, or are they indifferent about it? After giving students time to reflect, ask a few volunteers to share their positions and tell why they feel the way they do.

- Tell students that they will listen to a poem in which Armando expresses strong feelings about parent-teacher night. Have students listen as you read the poem aloud.

Comprehension Strategy: Drawing Conclusions

- Distribute copies of the poem or display it for the class.

- Remind students that sometimes when reading, they must draw conclusions about what the author is saying or thinking. Guide students in practicing this skill. Ask students questions and challenge them to give evidence from the poem to support their conclusions. For example: Does Armando consistently get good grades? Does Armando sometimes do things he is not proud of? Does Armando respect his mother? His teachers?

Standards-Based Skill Focus: Capitalization—Proper Nouns

- Have students find the terms *Bill of Rights* and *Constitution* in the poem. Ask students why these terms are capitalized. Then review that in addition to capitalizing the names of particular people, the names of particular places and things are proper nouns and are also capitalized.

- Distribute copies of page 96 for students to complete individually. After students complete the activity, ask a volunteer to read the story aloud. As a class, identify all the proper nouns in the story.

Vocabulary Word Study

- Have students find and highlight the following words in the poem: *severe*, *Rights*, *cruel*, *dictatorship*, and *persecution*. Have students reread the portion of text in which each word appears. If necessary, clarify for students the meaning of each word as it is used.

- Distribute copies of page 97, which checks students' understanding of these terms. You may choose to do the activity together as a group, or ask students to complete it individually.

TEACHER POLICE

by Armando Martí

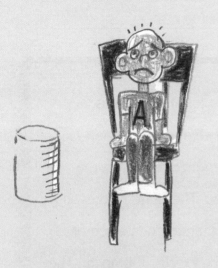

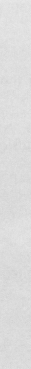

Oh, awful parent-teacher night,
how fearful I await you.
Tonight my mother learns the truth,
and that is why I hate you.

They'll tell her everything I said.
Her mood will turn severe.
They'll tell her everything I did.
She'll ground me for a year.

What about my privacy?
It's like I live in jail!
Does the Bill of Rights mean nothing?
Did the Constitution fail?

Our school's a cruel dictatorship!
Our teachers are secret police!
Won't someone find a way to make
this persecution cease?

Name:_____

Places and Things

Directions: Read the story below about early American history. Draw three lines under any letter that should be capitalized.

Example: Armando's great-great grandfather fought for pancho villa in the mexican revolution.

The united states of America prides itself on its freedom for all its citizens. This goes back to the late 1700s, when the country was newly formed. When the constitution was written, it contained a bill of rights designed to protect the freedom of citizens. Both documents are still in force today. The United States still has the three branches of government designed to ensure that no one person or group can control the government. The president heads the executive branch. The legislative, or law-making branch, consists of congress. At the top of the judicial branch is the supreme court and, below that, many other state and local courts.

America's founding fathers took great care in crafting the laws so that they would be fair and apply to everyone. Of course, over the last 200+ years, some things have been added and changes have been made, but the original constitution and bill of rights still stand as america's guidance. The original documents are still in their nation's capital—at the national archives in washington, d. c. It is amazing that although the world is so different now from how it was in thomas jefferson's time, americans can still count on the documents that have protected their rights and freedoms since the united states first declared itself an independent nation on july 4, 1776.

Name:_____

Teacher Police

I. Directions: Check your understanding of these words from the poem "Teacher Police" by answering the questions below.

| persecuted | cruel | dictatorship | rights | severe |

1. If something is *severe*, is it extremely bad or extremely good? _____

2. Are *rights* more like something you deserve or something you work for? _____

3. If someone is *cruel*, is he or she more likely to say something nice or something mean?

_____

4. In a *dictatorship*, do the people have a say or no say in how the government is run?

_____

5. If someone feels *persecuted*, would that person think he or she is being treated fairly or

unfairly? _____

• •

II. Directions: After reading Armando's complaints about school and parent-teacher night, would you agree or disagree with his claims? Write three sentences stating your position.

_____

_____

_____

Extension

Alone or with a partner, design and write a "Bill of Rights" for your class.

Snakehair Lady

In this poem, Armando characterizes his teacher as "Snakehair Lady," a reference to the mythological creature Medusa.

Making Connections

- Help students connect their own experiences to what they are about to read. Write the name *Medusa* on the board. Ask students to identify this character. If they do not know who she is, provide some prior knowledge, by offering this background. Explain that Greek mythology is filled with stories about supernatural beings. Medusa is a character who was a human, but because of her arrogance, was turned into a creature that had snakes for hair. She was supposed to have been so ugly that anyone who looked at her would turn to stone.

- Tell students that they will listen to a poem in which Armando describes his teacher as "Snakehair Lady"—comparing her to Medusa. Have students listen as you read the poem aloud.

Comprehension Strategy: Imagery

- Distribute copies of the poem or display it for the class.

- Explain that writers use carefully-chosen words to create vivid pictures for the readers. Ask students to find examples of Armando's use of imagery in the poem. Then invite students to draw the image that comes to their minds of Armando's teacher based on his description of her.

Standards-Based Skill Focus: Nouns Ending in *-sion* and *-tion*

- Write the following words *tense* and *agitate* on the board. Tell students that *tense* is a describing word and *agitate* is an action word. Next, ask students to look in the poem for words made from these roots (tension, agitation). Have students focus on the ending of each word. Explain that the endings *-sion* and *-tion* have been used to make the words *tense* and *agitate* into nouns, or naming words. The endings *-sion* and *-tion* usually mean "quality, act, or state of." For example, *tension* is the state of being tense; *agitation* is the state of being agitated.

- Distribute copies of page 100. Review the directions and examples together and then have students complete the activity individually.

Vocabulary Word Study

- Have students find and highlight the following words in the poem: *annihilate*, *tension*, *detention*, *agitation*, and *citation*. Have students reread the portion of text in which each word appears. If necessary, clarify the meaning of the word as it is used.

- Distribute copies of page 101, which checks their understanding of these terms. After reviewing the directions, have students complete the activity individually.

Snake hair LADY

by Armando Martí

The teacher is your friend—
it's what they always say,
but my teacher has the power
to annihilate my day.

"Where is your ID?" she says,
and I tighten up with tension.
'Cause if my teacher writes me up,
I'm headed for detention.

Or "Excuse me? Is that gum?"
And I feel the agitation.
If my teacher's feeling mean today,
she'll write me a citation.

She's as scary as the lady
with the hair all full of snakes.
'Cause your teacher is your friend
if you never make mistakes.

But if you break a single rule,
your heart will start to groan.
'Cause the anger in a teacher's eye
can turn you into stone.

Name:_____

It's a Noun

Directions: Each of the words below in the box is a noun made by adding *–sion* or *–tion* to a describing or action word. The endings *–sion* and *–tion* usually mean quality or state of, or act or result of. Study the example. Then write the noun that matches each description.

comprehension	infection	revision	education
agitation	complication	fascination	accusation
visitation	discussion	classification	reaction

Example:　　state of being tense: tension

1.　result of being infected: _____

2.　state of being complicated: _____

3.　act of visiting: _____

4.　result of reacting: _____

5.　state of being fascinated: _____

6.　result of revising: _____

7.　act of being educated: _____

8.　result of accusing: _____

9.　act of classifying: _____

10.　result of discussing: _____

11.　state of being agitated: _____

12.　result of comprehending: _____

Name:_____

Snakehair Lady

Directions: Check your understanding of the words from the poem "Snakehair Lady." Draw a line to match each term to its meaning. Then complete each sentence with one of the words.

1. annihilate — having anxious, worrisome, or uneasy feelings

2. tension — a form of punishment in which someone must remain behind after others have been dismissed or are engaged in other activities

3. detention — to defeat by completely destroying

4. agitation — an official acknowledgement; in law, an order to appear

5. citation — a state of anxiety usually accompanied by nervous shaking

6. When his teacher asks for his ID, Armando tightens up with _____.

7. Armando says that his teacher has the power to _____ his day.

8. He thinks if she's feeling mean, she will write him a _____.

9. That's why when she asks "Is that gum?" he feels _____.

10. Armando thinks the slightest slip will send him to _____.

Extension

Work with a partner to plan and practice a sketch showing what an exchange between Armando and his teacher might be like. Write out your sketch with speaking parts for Armando and the teacher. Choose your parts. After practicing several times, perform your skit for the whole class or a group of classmates.

Find the Common Denominator

When Alvin wrote about math, he wanted to understand the *why*. Armando just wants to get the problem solved the most efficient way possible. In this poem, he declares how to do that.

Making Connections

- Help students connect their own experiences to what they are about to read. Introduce the topic by asking if students agree that technology has eliminated the need for us to do many things by hand such as calculations, looking things up in a book, or handwriting a letter or note. Lead a brief discussion. Then ask students whether they think that today's students still need to learn the skills to do these tasks on their own—without the help of technology. Give students time to reflect and then allow time for discussion.

- Tell students that they will listen to a poem in which Armando expresses his opinion about having to do math problems by hand when a calculator is faster and more accurate. Have students listen as you read the poem aloud.

Comprehension Strategy: Summarize

- Distribute copies of the poem or display it for the class.

- Point out that Armando wrote four stanzas to make his point. Discuss the big idea of his poem.

- Challenge students to summarize the poem in one sentence. Allow time for students to write their sentences. Then call on a few students to share what they wrote. After hearing several ideas, ask students to write a new, revised one-sentence summary of the poem. Allow them to incorporate the ideas they heard into their new summaries.

Standards-Based Skill Focus: Syllabication

- Have students identify the number of syllables in various words from the poem and then divide them accordingly. Tell students that, in addition to having to do this "by hand," they may actually have to look up a word or two in the dictionary.

- Distribute copies of page 104 for students to complete individually.

Vocabulary Word Study

- Distribute copies of page 105, which challenges students to recognize misspelled words on their own—without the aide of a spell-checker.

- Remove any visible references to the poem. Tell students that this activity requires them to be human spell-checkers and that they must complete the activity without relying on anything but their own brainpower.

FIND THE COMMON DENOMINATOR

by Armando Martí

Finding the common denominator,
it's how we add up fractions,
but every time I do it,
I have very strange reactions.

It's such a waste of time.
I feel like such a fool.
I could add a zillion fractions
with a very simple tool.

Everybody's got one,
I've got one of my own—
this full-function calculator
right here in my phone.

I HAVE FOUND THE COMMON DENOMINATOR!
I shout with all my might:
THE EASY WAY IS ALWAYS WRONG!
THE HARD WAY'S ALWAYS RIGHT!

Name: _____

A Different Kind of Division

I. Directions: Write the number of syllables on the line next to each word.

common	_____	denominator	_____	fractions	_____	everybody	_____
function	_____	calculator	_____	reactions	_____	simple	_____

II. Directions: Write each word above on the correct mini-chart below. Divide the word into its syllable parts. The word *zillion* has been done for you as an example.

Two Syllables

1	2
zil	lion

Four Syllables

1	2	3	4

Three Syllables

1	2	3

Five Syllables

1	2	3	4	5

Name:_____

Find the Common Denominator

Directions: One of Armando's classmates liked his poem, so she decided to copy it into her notebook. The problem is that she made a few spelling mistakes, and since it was written by hand, she can't use the computer spell-checker. Your job is to be the human spell-checker. Find the misspelled word in each line. Underline it and then write it correctly on the line.

1. Find the common denomnator _____

2. It's howl we add up fractions _____

3. But every tim I do it _____

4. I have very stranj reactions _____

5. It's such a waist of time _____

6. I feel like sutch a fool, _____

7. I could add a zilliun fractions _____

8. With a very simpel tool _____

9. Everybudy's got one _____

10. Iv'e got one of my own _____

11. This full-funktion calculator _____

Extension

What do you think is the most useful technology tool and why?

Questions and Answers

Armando continues his theme of useless things about school in his next poem, in which he questions the need to memorize facts.

Making Connections

- Help students connect their own experiences to what they are about to read. Remind students that Armando thinks that many concepts taught in school are useless, such as doing math calculations by hand. In his next poem, he declares that memorizing facts will not do him much good. Ask students if they agree or disagree. Allow a few students to elaborate on their views.

- Ask students what kind of facts they think would be useful to know in the future. Offer examples such as knowing how to multiply or knowing the names of the states and where they are. Lead a brief discussion.

- Tell students that they will listen to a poem in which Armando questions having to memorize facts. Have students listen as you read the poem aloud.

Comprehension Strategy: Fluency—Pace and Tone

- Distribute copies of the poem or display it for the class.

- Have students highlight the lines in the poem in which ellipses appear. Explain their purpose in each case—to slow down or pause for emphasis, such as in *What…is the capital…of Alaska?* or to trail off as in *most state agencies are located where…?*

- Let students practice reading aloud using ellipses to guide their pace and tone.

Standards-Based Skill Focus: Homophones

- Use the poem's focus on capital cities as a springboard for reviewing homophones. Begin by writing *capital* and *capitol* on the board. Explain that these terms are commonly confused. Ask students which refers to a city (*capital*) and which to a building (*capitol*).

- Point out that many words sound the same, but they have different spellings and meanings. Remind students that these words are called *homophones*.

- Distribute copies of page 108. Review the directions and examples together. Then have students complete the activity individually. Afterward, review the answers as a group and have students check their own work.

Vocabulary Word Study

- Tell students that on the surface, Armando's poem seems to be convincing readers that students do not need to know such facts as the capital of every state, but by reading between the lines, it is clear that Armando knows a bit about capitals and geography in general.

- Use the vocabulary activity on page 109 not to focus on memorizing facts, but to read and recognize names of states, cities, and countries. Distribute copies of the activity page. Review the directions with students and have them complete the activity individually.

Questions and Answers

by Armando Martí

"What is the capital of Alaska?" he asked,
and though I could see he was looking at me,
I pretended not to notice.

"Mr. Martí," he growled,
"I'm talking to you.
What…is the capital…of Alaska?"

Now I couldn't remember the capital of Alaska,
but Mr. Shultz could easily go Darth Vader on me.
So I decided to give it a try,
which is when I discovered that Iceland is definitely
NOT…the capital of Alaska.

Now here's the thing—
I have not memorized all the capital city names,
but I've learned a lot about capital cities:

A state's capital city is not necessarily the state's largest city.
Capital cities tend to be located near the center of the state.
The governor's office is always in the capital city,
the state legislature always meets in the capital city,
and most state agencies are located where…?
In…the capital…city.

So be honest for a second,
and consider this suggestion,
Might I give a better answer
if he'd asked a better question?

And which will serve me better
when the future is at hand:
the facts they made me memorize
or the thoughts I understand?

Name:_____

Not the Same

Directions: Read the homophones and their meanings. Then challenge yourself to write one sentence using both homophones. See the examples below.

Examples:

> 1. **capital**: the city or seat of government of a state or country
>   **capitol**: the building in Washington, D.C., in which Congress meets
>   The capitol is located in Washington, D.C., our nation's capital.
> 2. **principal**: the head of a school; chief
>   **principle**: a basic law, rule, or standard
>   The principal issued a list of principles by which the school would operate.

1. **aloud**: in a way that can be heard   **allowed**: permitted

   _____

   _____

2. **weather**: climate   **whether**: if

   _____

   _____

3. **stationary**: in a fixed position   **stationery**: writing paper

   _____

   _____

4. **waste**: trash; unusable part   **waist**: middle of the body

   _____

   _____

Name: _____

Questions and Answers

Directions: In his poem, Armando raised the question of whether it is important to know the capital of each state. It may or may not be, but it certainly is important that you can read and recognize the names of states, major cities, and countries (and know that they begin with capital letters). Below are the names of 24 places for you to identify as a city, state, or country. Write *city*, *state*, or *country* next to each place.

1. London _____

2. New Orleans _____

3. France _____

4. San Francisco _____

5. Mexico _____

6. California _____

7. Florida _____

8. Chicago _____

9. Kenya _____

10. Tokyo _____

11. Egypt _____

12. Australia _____

13. Atlanta _____

14. Colorado _____

15. Rio de Janiero _____

16. Hawaii _____

17. Washington, D.C. _____

18. Iraq _____

19. Rome _____

20. Brazil _____

Extension

You may not have memorized the capital of every country, but you should at least know the capital of your own country. Write the name of the capital of your country.

The Flame

In his final poem, Armando lives up to his nickname—"The Flame"—first by continuing to express his opinion on burning issues and also by his burning desire to learn.

Making Connections

- Help students connect their own experiences to what they are about to read. Write the term *accountable* on the board. Ask students to speculate on what it means. After a few suggestions, provide this definition: taking responsibility for something and the consequences of it. Share a few examples.

- Explain that in school, teachers and administrators are accountable for students' learning and progress. One way to measure this is through testing, which requires students to demonstrate what they know. Teachers and administrators have to prove that students are acquiring the needed skills.

- Tell students that they will listen to a poem in which Armando complains of too much testing. Have students listen as you read the poem aloud.

Comprehension Strategy: Author's Purpose—Persuade

- Distribute copies of the poem or display it for the class.

- Remind students that authors write for different purposes, such as to entertain, inform, or persuade. Ask students what they think Armando's intended purpose was for writing this poem and why.

Standards-Based Skill Focus: Responding to Informational Text

- Distribute copies of the page 112. Have students skim the tips and then ask if the purpose of the text is to entertain, inform, or persuade. After establishing that it is informational text, read through the tips as a group.

- Direct students to reread the text on their own and then answer the questions at the bottom of the page. You may want to revisit the activity after everyone is finished to invite students to share their responses to the text.

Vocabulary Word Study

- Make sure students have a copy of the poem or can reference a displayed copy. Then distribute copies of page 113 to students.

- Explain that Armando used several colorful expressions in his poem to convey his "fiery" passion about the topic of testing. Tell students to find the figurative phrases he used to replace literal meanings.

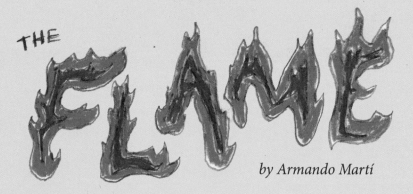

THE FLAME

by Armando Martí

Dear parents, principals, and presidents,
you're trying to do your best,
but what are you accomplishing
by drowning us in tests?

It's all our teacher thinks about,
her number one concern.
We work so hard on taking tests,
we don't have time to learn.

And I know it's not her fault.
I think she hates it, too.
But the big dogs think it's right,
so it's what she has to do.

Ask the scholars! Check the facts!
It's not helping us at all!
Can anybody hear me?
Am I talking to a wall?

Curiosity and passion!
A hunger for the truth!
Now's our time to get it,
in this moment of our youth.

So…
Dear parents, principals, and presidents,
please accept this invitation:
Refocus the aim! Ignite the flame!
Believe in education!

Name:_____

This Is Not a Test

Directions: Chances are that you have had to take plenty of tests—multiple choice, true-false, and maybe even essays. Although Armando would be happy if he never had to take another test, the reality is that tests are part of school and learning. Here are some tips that may help you do better on tests. Read the tips and then answer the questions below.

Test-Taking Tips

1. Look over the whole test before you begin. Read the directions carefully. Make sure you understand what you are being asked to do.

2. Complete the questions that you are sure of first. Then go back to the ones you are not as sure of.

3. Don't allow yourself to spend too much time on any one question. This may prevent you from being able to finish the test. If you are stuck, move on. Then if you have time, come back to the troublesome question.

4. For multiple-choice questions, be sure to read all of the answers before choosing. If you are not sure which is the correct one, see if you can eliminate a choice that you know is not correct. This will narrow your choices and increase your chance of choosing the correct one.

5. As you read a question, look for words such as *always*, *never*, *none*, and *all*. These often (but not always) eliminate an answer as correct or true.

6. If you have time at the end of a test, change an answer only if you are sure and have a good reason for doing so. If you chose an answer that you were unsure of, more often that not, your first choice will have a better chance of being right.

---

1. Which tip did you find to be most helpful? Write the number. _____

2. Tip 5 gives some words to look for. Why do you think these words more often than

   not eliminate an answer as correct or true? _____

   _____

3. It is common for students to get an answer wrong simply because they hurried

   through the test. What can you do to avoid this? _____

4. When should you change an answer on a test?_____

   _____

   _____

Name:_____

The Flame

Directions: Armando's poem "The Flame" contains several phrases that don't mean exactly what the words say. These colorful expressions add "fire" to his writing. Perhaps that is why his nickname is "The Flame." Use the poem to find six ways Armando chose to use colorful phrases instead of plain, boring explanations.

1. Instead of just saying that students are given a lot of tests, what colorful expression does Armando use? _____

2. Instead of just saying that it is the school administrators who make the decisions, what colorful name does he give them? _____

   _____

3. Instead of just complaining that no one is listening to him, what phrase does Armando use? _____

4. Instead of just saying that the time to do something is while we are young, what does Armando call the time? _____

   _____

5. Instead of just saying that students would like to learn the truth, what colorful expression conveys this? _____

6. Instead of just suggesting that the adults should start getting students excited again about education, what phrase does he use that compares excitement to fire? _____

Extension

Armando's poem was intended to persuade adults to give fewer tests and spend more time on learning. What evidence did he give to support his argument? How could he improve his argument so that it is more convincing?

Veronica "Queen of the Dead" Page

Here, Shaneka introduces us to Veronica Page, also known as "Queen of the Dead." We find out that she is unique in several ways. She has an interesting exterior, but she also has a unique perspective.

Making Connections

- Help students connect their own experiences to what they will read. Ask students to take time to reflect on what the clothing says about the people who wear it. Do people's clothes make it easy for others to predict their personalities or are clothes just the exterior shell?

- Tell students to listen as you read the introduction to Veronica Page.

Comprehension Strategy: Critical Thinking—Questioning

- Distribute copies of the introduction or display it for the class.

- Remind students that this introduction sets the stage for the entire set of poems they will be reading by Veronica. Ask students questions to ensure their understanding of Veronica and both her exterior and interior personas. How does Veronica look on the exterior? How does her exterior match or not match her name? What is Veronica like on the interior? How does her interior match or not match her nickname? What kinds of poems do you think Veronica will write?

Standards-Based Skill Focus: Pronouns

- Write the word *pronoun* on the board. Remind students that pronouns take the place of nouns. Work together to create a list of pronouns.

- Write the following sentence on the board: *The class liked the field trip so much that the class wanted to go again.* Ask students which words in that sentence could be replaced with pronouns. Work together to rewrite the sentence.

- Distribute copies of the skill activity on page 116, which focuses on using pronouns. Have students complete the activity individually or in pairs.

Vocabulary Word Study

- Tell students that *character* describes what a person is like. There are some words that describe a person's character better than others.

- Ask students to think about what they know about Veronica. Ask if one of these words describes her better than the others: *bossy, grouchy,* or *unique.* Discuss with students why, of these three words, *unique* best describes Veronica. Have students point to evidence in the introduction that helps prove their points.

- Distribute copies of page 117, which focuses on identifying additional character traits for Veronica as well as the students in your class. Have students complete the activity individually.

VERONICA Queen of the Dead PAGE

Veronica Page is over the top. She actually cultivates an appearance she calls "vampire-chic." It's not just that she dyes her hair purple and wears long black dresses. She actually calls her bedroom "the tomb," her bed "the coffin," and in her purse she has these plastic vampire fangs that fit perfectly over her real teeth and look real enough to give you the chills. It happened when we were in fifth grade. One day she was blonde-haired, blue-eyed, spring-dresses Veronica Page, and the next day, she was Veronica—Queen of the Dead!

The key to understanding Veronica is that she's different. And I'm not just talking about the vampire thing; that's all an act. I think it makes her feel safe, like if she looks dangerous, people will keep their distance. I'm talking about the real Veronica, her inner thinking; she's different. You may have heard people use the phrase "thinking out of the box"? Well for Veronica, there never was a box. She's really smart, she reads constantly, and all of her thinking, on every subject, is totally out of the box.

So with Veronica, what you see is a kind of false front, which is ironic because she's constantly on the attack against things that are fake. She once told me that "ninety percent of what people say is a collection of half-truths, exaggerations, and lies." I asked her about the remaining ten percent. She hesitated, a kind of sad smile on her face. Then she shifted into her vampire act, and using her hissing vampire voice, she said, "They're utter mindless clichés. It's why I suck their blood."

So Veronica's pretty much an original thinker, which is why I saved her for last. I hope you'll like her as much as we do.

Name: _____

Replace It

Directions: Read the sentences below. Replace the blanks with pronouns from the word bank. Hint: Pronouns may be used more than once or not at all.

he	she	him	his	it
I	they	we	our	

1. The slam poetry team at our school has five members in _____.

2. _____ leader is Shaneka.

3. Another member is Devin. _____ nickname is "I'm-OK-You're-OK." _____ is easygoing.

4. Alvin "Nerd-One" Lofton is another member. _____ is a self-proclaimed nerd.

5. Armando's nickname is "El Fuego." _____ likes to question authority.

6. Finally, the "Queen of the Dead" is Veronica. _____ is an original thinker.

7. Together, _____ make up our school's team.

8. We love poetry. _____ team finished third in a competition. _____ hope to finish first next year.

Name: _____

Veronica "Queen of the Dead" Page

I. Directions: Read each of the character traits in the box below. Highlight any words you think describe Veronica based on what Shaneka shares in the introduction. Then identify the three traits you think most identify Veronica's character and use the words to complete the sentence.

Character Traits

nervous	sad	sneaky	agreeable	cautious	secretive
creepy	fake	vain	outspoken	calm	fearful
lonely	friendly	envious	fierce	sensitive	stubborn
confident	polite	pushy	opinionated	cheerful	moody
gentle	serious	grouchy	studious	logical	deep
funny	nosy	arrogant	distant	inquisitive	aggressive
bossy	timid	nervous	generous	popular	grouchy
tough	loyal	lazy	restless	indifferent	observant
rebellious	smart	silly	optimistic	insightful	daring

Veronica is _____, _____, and _____.

II. Directions: Now circle any words in the box above that you think describe you. Then identify the three traits you think most identify your character, and use the words to complete the sentence.

I am _____, _____, and _____.

Extension

Make a list of character traits that are not listed above. Rewrite the sentence you completed to include words that describe you, if appropriate.

Vampire Friends

Veronica's first poem, "Vampire Friends," is all about feelings. Veronica shares how others feel about the way she dresses, as well as how that makes her feel.

Making Connections

- Help students connect their own experiences to what they are about to read. Ask students to think of a time when someone said something about their appearance that hurt their feelings. Discuss whether it matters that the person who shares his or her comments is a close friend, an acquaintance, or a stranger? Allow time for students to reflect and then have students share their thoughts and experiences in small groups.

- Tell students that they will listen to a poem in which Veronica is upset because of some comments her peers are making about her appearance. Ask them to listen to how the comments affect her. Have students listen as you read the poem aloud.

Comprehension Strategy: Using Punctuation for Fluency

- Distribute copies of the poem or display it for the class.

- Remind students that punctuation marks are there as a guide on how to read the passage so that it makes sense and flows. Punctuation marks also help the reader know the intended voice of the passage and how to express it. Review the voicing for punctuation markings.

- Have students practice reading the poem several times using the punctuation marks to guide their flow and expression.

Standards-Based Skill Focus: Verbal Techniques—Quotations

- Remind students that quotation marks show the exact words a person says. Reread the poem to students without changing your voice when quotation marks are used in the text. Tell students that reading the poem this way does not help listeners easily identify when a new character is speaking in the poem.

- Distribute copies of page 120. Tell students that this page will provide them with practice using their voices to create characters with the direct quotations in the poem. Have students complete the activity as a class.

Vocabulary Word Study

- Have students find and highlight the following words in the poem: *reflection, insensitive, fangs, personal, chic, egomania, chatter, Transylvania*. Have students reread the portions of text in which the words appear. If necessary, clarify for students the meaning of each word as it is used.

- Distribute copies of page 121, which offers a fun puzzle to reinforce learning of the words. Allow students to complete the activity in pairs or individually.

Vampire Friends

by Veronica Page

It's those who are close
who will hurt you the most,
like my friend Tearney:

"Girl, don't look at me like that," she said.
"Like what?" I asked.
"You know," she said,
"that vampire stare, like you're about to bite my neck."

Or my friend Juan:

"Veronica," he said,
"I've figured out why your hair is always a mess.
You don't make a reflection when you look in the mirror."

How can they be so insensitive?
Just because my clothes are all black,
I dye my hair purple,
and I carry with me,
at all times,
a very cool pair of Hollywood vampire fangs.
It's my personal style.
I call it vampire-chic.

But it's those who are close
who will hurt you the most,
as they deal with their own egomania.
While they chatter and chat, I'll turn into a bat,
and fly back to my dear Transylvania.

Name:_____

Vocalize It

Directions: Below are the direct quotations from Veronica's poem "Vampire Friends." Follow the steps below to help identify who is saying what. Then practice reading the lines, using your voice to express the character's feelings.

Steps for Fluent Reading

1. Use a yellow crayon or marker to underline the exact words that Veronica says in the poem. **Hint:** In the lines below, Veronica is identified by the word *I*. Her exact words are the words in the quotation marks.

2. Use an orange crayon or marker to underline the exact words of Tearney.

3. Use a green crayon or marker to underline the exact words of Juan.

4. Look at the word that identifies the tone next to each line below. Practice reading the lines using that tone in your voice.

5. Read the line using other tones such as scared, joyful, all-knowing, or timid.

6. Decide which tone you think most accurately portrays the author's intent for the words.

7. After you have practiced, show someone you know—a friend or family member—how well you can read these lines with expression.

Tone	Quote	Other Tones
Annoyed	"Girl, don't look at me like that," she said.	_____
Perplexed	"Like what?" I asked.	_____
Annoyed	"You know," she said, "that vampire stare, like you're about to bite my neck."	_____
All-knowing	"Veronica," he said, "I've figured out why your hair is always a mess. You don't make a reflection when you look in the mirror."	_____

Name:_____

Vampire Friends

Directions: Here's a crossword puzzle with a bit of a twist. Rather than listing clues as across and down, they appear within sentences. You can use context clues in the sentences to help you figure out the missing word to fill in the puzzle. All the words can be found in the poem "Vampire Friends."

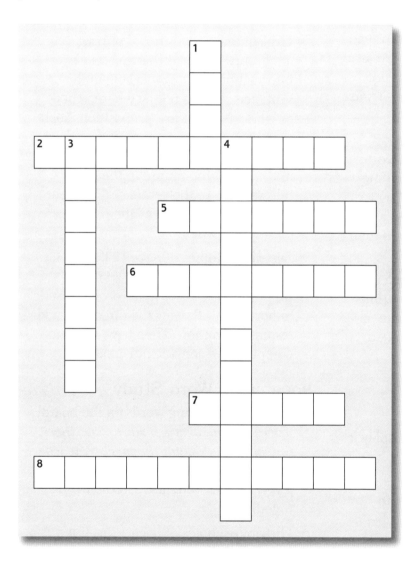

Clues:

Her *3 down* prevented her from wanting to help other people.

The snake's *7 across* allowed venomous poison to go into its bite victim.

I could see my *2 across* when I looked into the pond.

Ripped jeans are in style and oh, so *1 down*.

It is rumored that vampires live in *4 down*.

My laptop is my *6 across* computer.

The *5 across* in the classroom prevented me from hearing the message on the loud speaker.

It is *8 across* to talk about your pet when someone else's has just died.

Extension

Here's a chance to express your opinion about something at school. Did you like or dislike doing this puzzle? Did the unusual form make it more difficult or more fun?

The Joy of Youth

In her second poem, Veronica sounds a bit like Armando as she complains about how adults "so quickly forget" what it is like to be in school.

Making Connections

- Help students connect their own experiences to what they are about to read. Ask students whether they have heard an adult claim that being young means not having a care or worry in the world. Then ask how many agree with that claim.

- Discuss what the phrase *"a walk in the park"* means. Once students have established that it means that something is easy, ask how many think that going to school and being a kid in general is "a walk in the park." Invite students to share their opinions and ideas.

- Tell students that they will listen to a poem in which Veronica is upset because adults think that being a kid is "a walk in the park." Have students listen as you read the poem aloud.

Comprehension Strategy: Main Idea and Details

- Distribute copies of the poem or display it for the class.

- Explain that stating the main idea and important details is a good way to summarize and remember what has been read. Write the following on the board: *Adults think kids have no stress or worries, but they are wrong.* Tell students that this is the main idea of Veronica's poem. Ask students to copy it as the topic sentence of a paragraph about the poem. Students must then complete the paragraph with details. Give them sentence starters, such as *For example, In addition,* and *Finally.*

Standards-Based Skill Focus: Prepositional Phrases

- Explain that prepositional phrases are groups of words that give more information about something in the sentence, such as telling where, when, or what. Name a few prepositions such as *in, on, at, of, with,* or *to.* Offer these examples: In the sentence "He jumped in the pool," the phrase *in the pool* tells where. In the sentence "He went swimming after dinner," the phrase *after dinner* tells when.

- Distribute copies of page 124. Explain that this activity highlights some prepositional phases that Veronica used in her poem. Review the directions and example together. Then have students complete the activity individually.

Vocabulary Word Study

- Write the following words on the board: *worry, world, every, hear, where, there, universal, curricular, homework, teacher, ever, overpowering, pressure, park,* and *forget.* Have students read the words together.

- Distribute copies of page 125. Tell students it focuses on spelling words that contain a vowel + *r.* Review the directions and then have students complete the activity individually.

The Joy of Youth

by *Veronica Page*

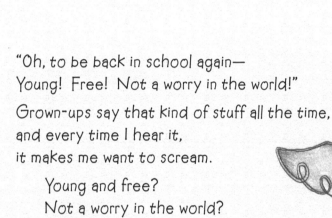

"Oh, to be back in school again—
Young! Free! Not a worry in the world!"

Grown-ups say that kind of stuff all the time,
and every time I hear it,
it makes me want to scream.

Young and free?
Not a worry in the world?
I don't know where they went to school,
but at my school, there ain't nothin' free about being young,
and worrying is our universal extracurricular activity.
Homework! Teachers! Projects! Tests!
And the ever-present, overpowering pulse of peer pressure!

Youth is not a walk in the park.
It's pain! And stress! And sweat!
Young and free? Not a worry in the world?
How quickly they forget.

Name:_____

Prepositional Phrases

Directions: Below are lines from Veronica's poem "The Joy of Youth" that contain prepositional phrases. The preposition is in italics, and the whole phrase is in bold. Copy each prepositional phrase under the category it answers—*Where* or *What*. For example, the phrase *of Youth* in the title tells what joy, so it is written under the *What* category.

Lines from "The Joy of Youth"
The Joy *of* **Youth**
"Oh, to be back *in* **school** again—Young! Free! Not a worry *in* **the world**!"
Grown-ups say that kind *of* **stuff** all the time,
and every time I hear it,
it makes me want to scream.
At **my school,** there ain't nothin' free *about* **being young.**
And the ever-present, overpowering pulse *of* **peer pressure**!
Youth is not a walk *in* **the park**.

Where	_____ _____ _____ _____
What	_____of youth_____ _____ _____ _____

Name:_____

The Joy of Youth

Directions: You may not have noticed, but there are many words in Veronica's poem that contain a vowel + the letter *r*. These can be tricky because the *r* sometimes affects the vowel sound. Write the missing vowel—*a*, *e*, *i*, *o*, or *u*—in each blank below.

1. Young! Free! Not a w___rry in the w___rld!

   Grown-ups say that kind of stuff all the time,

   and ev___ry time I he___r it,

   it makes me want to scream.

2. I don't know wh___re they went to school,

   but at my school, th___re ain't nothin' free about being young,

   and w___rrying is our univ___rsal extrac___rricul___r activity.

   Homew___rk! Teach___rs! Projects! Tests!

   And the ev___r-present, ov___rpow___ring pulse of pe___r press___re!

3. Youth is not a walk in the p___rk.

   It's pain! And stress! And sweat!

   Young and free? Not a w___rry in the w___rld?

   How quickly they f___rget.

Extension

Is being young and in school more of "a walk in the park" or like being "between a rock and a hard place"? Explain your answer.

Sprained Heart

Although Veronica puts on a tough exterior, in this poem, she reveals her vulnerability.

Making Connections

- Help students connect their own experiences to what they are about to read. Ask students to think of a time when they felt left behind or when someone that they thought of as a friend hurt their feelings. Give an example such as, "One Halloween, I was busy putting on my costume, and my friends left without me." Give students time to reflect and then call on students to share their experiences. Encourage students to tell how they felt as well as a result of what happened.

- Tell students that they will listen to a poem in which Veronica's feelings are hurt because her friends left her behind. Have students listen as you read the poem aloud.

Comprehension Strategy: Making Inferences

- Distribute copies of the poem or display it for the class.

- Tell students that an *inference* is a conclusion made about something not directly stated in the text. For example, the poem begins with a reply from Veronica's father. The poem does not directly state that Veronica told her father what happened, but readers can infer that she did because of his reply.

- Ask students to reread the second stanza of the poem. Then ask students to offer their ideas about who "they" are and what in the poem led them to that inference.

Standards-Based Skill Focus: Identifying Verbs

- Remind students that *verbs* are words that show action or being. Action verbs are often easy to spot in a sentence. For example, in the sentence *Veronica wrote a poem*, the action is *wrote*.

- Explain that "being verbs" are sometimes more difficult to identify. Challenge students to identify the verb in this sentence: *It's about hurt feelings*. Explain that, in this case, the verb is part of the contraction *it's*, which means "it is." The contraction *it's* contains the subject—*it*, and the verb—*is*.

- Provide students additional practice with identifying verbs, including multiple uses of the contraction *it's*. Distribute copies of page 128 to students. Allow students to complete the activity individually and then review it together.

Vocabulary Word Study

- Tell students that developing a strong vocabulary involves more than just learning new word meanings. It also means understanding how words are related.

- Distribute copies of page 129. Read the directions aloud and then ask how the ending *-less* affects the meaning of a word (changes it to mean "without"). Finally, have students complete the activity individually.

by Veronica Page

"It's not the end of the world," my daddy said,
and I know he means well,
but sometimes he doesn't have a clue.

Of course, it's not the end of the world,
but last night they were supposed to call,
and we were supposed to go the mall together,
but they didn't call,
and they went to the mall without me,
and there's nothing I can do about it,
and it's not the end of the world,
but it hurts.
It really hurts.

Last summer, I sprained my ankle
and you know how that can feel,
so I kept it cold, and lo and behold,
the sprain began to heal.

So Daddy, thanks for trying to help,
but it's really no time for advice.
I just wish that they could find a way
to pack a heart in ice.

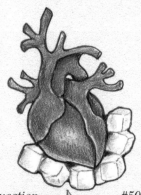

Name:_____

Finding Verbs

Directions: Below are phrases from Veronica's poem "Sprained Heart." Fill in the bubble that identifies the verb in each line. Remember, verbs can be hidden in contractions!

1. He means well.　　　　　　　○ he　　　○ means　　　○ well

2. It's not the end of the world.　　○ it　　　○ is　　　○ end

3. They went to the mall without me.　○ went　　○ mall　　○ without

4. It really hurts.　　　　　　　○ it　　　○ really　　○ hurts

5. Last summer, I sprained my ankle.　○ last　　○ sprained　○ ankle

6. I kept it cold.　　　　　　　○ I　　　○ kept　　　○ cold

7. Thanks for trying to help.　　　○ thanks　○ trying　　○ help

8. It's really no time for advice.　　○ is　　　○ time　　　○ advice

9. Pack a heart in ice.　　　　　　○ in　　　○ heart　　○ pack

Name:_____

Sprained Heart

Directions: The ending *-less* means "without". Write the word for each meaning below. Form the word by adding the ending *-less* to each italicized base word.

1. without a *clue* _____

2. without *breath* _____

3. without a *border* _____

4. without *care* _____

5. without *taste* _____

6. without *guilt* _____

7. without a *flaw* _____

8. without *harm* _____

9. without *hope* _____

10. without *sleep* _____

11. without a *cord* _____

12. without *worth* _____

13. without *sense*_____

14. without *power*_____

15. without *hair* _____

16. without a *goal* _____

17. without *odor* _____

18. without *color* _____

19. without a *home* _____

20. without a *friend* _____

21. without an *end*_____

22. without *fear* _____

Extension

Choose five of the words you created. Use each of them in a sentence. Example: Veronica felt that her dad meant well, but that he was clueless.

Private Poison

In this poem, Veronica switches to a whimsical mood as she humorously describes how she got poison ivy in a "private" place.

Making Connections

- Help students connect their own experiences to what they are about to read. Ask students to think of a time when they were going somewhere or in a place where there was no bathroom and they needed to go. Then have students generate words that describe how that felt.

- Ask if anyone has ever had poison ivy or another kind of itchy rash. Then have students generate words that describe that feeling. Record students' descriptive words on the board for both questions. Save the list for use in the skill activity.

- Tell students that they will listen to a poem in which Veronica describes how she happened to get poison ivy in an unmentionable place. Have students listen as you read the poem aloud.

Comprehension Strategy: Generating Questions

- Distribute copies of the poem or display it for the class.

- Remind students that one way to check their understanding is by answering questions about what they read. Remind students about the 5 Ws—*who/m, what, where, when,* and *why.*

- Divide students into pairs. Challenge them to write five questions about the poem based on the 5 Ws. Then have students exchange questions with their partners and answer their partners' questions orally or in writing.

Standards-Based Skill Focus: Differentiating Adjectives from Adverbs

- Review the list of words generated in the Making Connections activity. Point out to students that these words all describe how something felt. Words that describe actions or feelings are called *adverbs.* Erase the list.

- Explain to students that now they are going to focus on adjective words that describe people, places, and objects and usually tell which, what kind, or how many. Ask students to generate words that might describe each of these things: *rash, farm, a grove of trees.*

- Distribute copies of page 132, which contains a copy of the first three stanzas of Veronica's poem. Explain that the bold words in the poem are nouns that name things. Students must find the adjectives, or words used to describe these things. Have students complete the activity individually or in pairs.

Vocabulary Word Study

- Use the activity on page 133 to enrich students' vocabularies with adjectives. Remind students that adjectives tell which, what kind, or how many.

- Distribute copies of page 133. Read and review the adjectives that appear on the page. Then have students supply nouns for each adjective.

by Veronica Page

I have a terrible rash,
and no, I can't show you,
because it's in a very private place.

It happened on our field trip.
We went to a dairy farm way out in the country,
and on the way home, on the bus,
just when I realized I needed to use the toilet,
a flat tire.
So there I was—
stranded on a road in the middle of a forest,
no chance of finding a potty.

Eventually, nature's call got so strong,
I was forced to go off on my own in search of relief,
and I found it—
    a little grove of lovely trees
    and everywhere around,
    bright green vines that intertwined
    to weave a wall of protection.
Peaceful, private, perfect.

And that is where it happened,
in that very private place,
and that is why my poison ivy
isn't on my face.

Name: _____

Finding Adjectives

Directions: Below is part of Veronica's poem "Private Poison." The bold words you see are *nouns*—names of things. Find any *adjectives* used to describe each thing. List them on the lines at the right. **Hint:** Look for words that tell which, what kind, or how many. One of the adjectives is used twice.

Private Poison

I have a terrible **rash**,
and no, I can't show you,
because it's in a very private **place**.

It happened on our field **trip**.
We went to a dairy **farm** way out in the
country,
and on the way home, on the bus,
just when I realized I needed to use the
toilet,
a flat **tire**.
So there I was—
stranded on a road in the middle of a forest,
no chance of finding a potty.

Eventually, nature's call got so strong,
I was forced to go off on my own in search
of relief,
and I found it—
a little **grove** of lovely **trees**
and everywhere around,
bright green **vines** that intertwined
to weave a **wall** of protection.
Peaceful, private, perfect.

1. _____

2. _____

3. _____

4. _____

5. _____

6. _____

7. _____

8. _____

9. _____

10. _____

11. _____

Name:_____

Private Poison

Directions: Read the adjective in bold. Then write in two different nouns (naming words) that the adjective could be used to describe. The first one is done for you as an example.

1. a **terrible** ____rash____   a **terrible** ____storm____

2. the **shortest** _____   the **shortest** _____

3. a **red** _____   a **red** _____

4. my **best** _____   my **best** _____

5. a **few** _____   a **few** _____

6. a **delicious** _____   a **delicious** _____

7. a **sparkling** _____   a **sparkling** _____

8. an **enormous** _____   an **enormous** _____

9. a **powerful** _____   a **powerful** _____

10. an **impatient** _____   an **impatient** _____

11. a **terrific** _____   a **terrific** _____

12. an **empty** _____   an **empty** _____

Extension

Copy the following sentence on a separate sheet of paper. Then fill in adjectives that would make sense in the blanks: While on a _____ trip, out of the _____ window I spotted the most _____ bird I'd ever seen circling in the _____, _____ sky.

Where Eagles Fly

In her final poem, Veronica seems to have softened up by writing about nature's beauty, but then she introduces a shocking twist—something quite the opposite!

Making Connections

- Help students connect their own experiences to what they are about to read. Tell students that they will be reading a poem about the pros and cons of camping. Call on any volunteers to explain what camping is like and/or what they know about ticks.

- Make four columns on the board. Label the first two *What We Know* and *What We Want to Know*. Ask students to suggest what to record in the first column. Then ask students what they want to know about ticks. Record their responses in the second column.

- Tell students that they will listen to a poem in which Veronica describes her camping experience. Have students listen as you read the poem aloud.

Comprehension Strategy: KWLS Organizer

- Tell students that a good way to analyze something they read is to organize it on a chart or other graphic representation, such as the KWLS organizer you've started.

- Review the information you recorded on the board under the headings *What We Know* and *What We Want to Know*. After reading the poem, label the third column on the board *What We Learned* and ask students for input on what to write in that column. Then label the final column *What We Still Want to Know*. Record students' ideas.

Standards-Based Skill Focus: Making Judgments Based on Text

- Use the activity on page 136 to give students the opportunity to make judgments based on what they read. Divide the class into small groups. Distribute one copy of the page to each group. Explain the terms *pro* and *con*.

- Have students work in their groups to come up with possible pros and cons of camping in the woods. Give them time to discuss and record their answers. Then ask one person from each group to share the group's responses.

Vocabulary Word Study

- Explain to students that one useful tool for understanding and learning vocabulary is to use a *thesaurus*—a tool that lists synonyms (words that mean the same) and antonyms (words that mean the opposite). If possible, demonstrate using a printed thesaurus or the thesaurus function on a computer word-processing program.

- Distribute copies of page 137. Review the directions together and then have students complete the activity individually.

Where Eagles Fly

by Veronica Page

Yesterday, way out in the woods,
the air so fresh and clean,
it was there I saw the most beautiful sight
my eyes have ever seen.

A golden eagle that soared with a power
mere words could never convey.
It carved giant circles in the sky
and slowly flew away.

Then all night long in my sleeping bag,
I dreamed of that beautiful sight,
but early this morning, when I opened my eyes,
my leg wasn't feeling quite right.

That's when I saw it, there on my foot,
right there with the toe-cheese and crud—
a big... fat... bulging... tick...
all bloated up with blood.

There's a lesson here, I said to myself,
it's one of life's little tricks—
if you want to walk where eagles fly,
you must learn to live with the ticks.

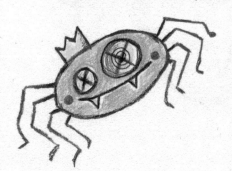

tix PLAY trix!

Name:_____

Two Sides to Everything

Directions: Your job is to brainstorm several *pros* (positive aspects) and several *cons* (negative aspects) of camping in the woods. Draw upon your personal experience, the experience of others, or just what you imagine it would be like to make your judgments.

Camping in the Woods

Pros	Cons

tix
PLAY
trix!

Name:_____

Where Eagles Fly

Directions: Each word in the left column is a word from the poem "Where Eagles Fly." Write a synonym for each word. Use a thesaurus if you need help. Then use the word in a sentence or phrase.

Word	Synonym	Sentence or Phrase Using the Word
beautiful		
convey		
giant		
early		
bulging		
bloated		
walk		
fly		

Extension

On a large sheet of paper, make a KWLS chart about eagles, ticks, or another animal. Use books, encyclopedias, or websites to find out more about the animal and to fill in the "L" (What I Learned) section of the chart.

Answer Key

Page 20

1. pro-nounced
2. cap-tain
3. in-volved
4. com-pe-ti-tion
5. col-lec-tion
6. en-ter-tained
7. prac-tice
8. class-room
9. per-for-man-ces
10. whis-pers
11. captain
12. collection
13. entertained
14. involved
15. competition

Page 21

ir Words—thirteen, giraffe, chirp, sir, circus

er Words—entertained, thunder, yesterday, ruler, sister

1. ruler
2. yesterday
3. circus
4. chirp
5. thunder

Page 24

1. F	9. O
2. O	10. F
3. O	11. O
4. O	12. O
5. O	13. F
6. F	14. O
7. O	15. O
8. O	16. F

Page 25

1. better	9. hard
2. too much	10. rather
3. should	11. may
4. probably	12. extremely
5. worst	13. important
6. good	14. seems
7. certain	15. believe
8. good	16. shouldn't

Page 28

1. birthday is	7. future is
2. twelve is	8. I am
3. it is	9. That is
4. does not	10. I would
5. do not	11. There is
6. We are	12. it will

Page 29

I. 90, 14, 35, 10, 56, 63, 40, 13, 2, 15, 81, 29, 10, 70, 100, 80, 18, 75, 0, 19, 1,000, 60, 17, 24

II.

1. twelve
2. one hundred ten
3. thirty-nine
4. forty thousand
5. twenty-two
6. eight hundred
7. ninety-four
8. one million
9. seventy-three
10. six hundred one

Page 32

Students' summary sentences will vary, but they should include the main idea of each stanza.

Page 33

me and *see*—Italy, guarantee, degree, debris, disagree

chill and *will*—fulfill, Brazil, spill, refill, until

Students' rhyming words will vary.

1. No, rhyming words do not have to have the same spelling patterns at the end of the words.
2. There are no words that rhyme with vague and plague. (Technically there are some other words, although they are not widely used.)

Page 36

Metaphors should be underlined as follows. Students' explanations may vary. Suggested explanations are included.

1. in hot water; in trouble
2. a disaster area; a mess
3. a pig; person who eats too much
4. food for thought; something to think about
5. music to my ears; good to hear
6. a breeze; easy

Page 37

1. metaphor
2. actual
3. metaphor
4. metaphor
5. actual
6. metaphor
7. metaphor
8. actual

Page 40

1. so the bus left without him.
2. therefore school was canceled.
3. I didn't invite her to my party.
4. the water overflowed onto the floor.
5. the factory cut its production.
6. that there was not room for everyone.
7. resulted in him getting an infection.
8. then we have to finish it for homework.
9. so I ended up having to pay a fine.
10. Dad gets annoyed and makes me turn it down.

Answer Key (cont.)

Page 41
1. little
2. tremble
3. terrible
4. nickel
5. double
6. nibble
7. giggle
8. cancel
9. camel
10. single
11. angel
12. table
13. level
14. trickle
15. hotel
16. travel
17. candle
18. bagel
19. needle
20. possible
21. channel
22. article
23. duel
24. label

Page 44
Down
1. showed
2. think
4. realize
5. make
7. dealt

Across
3. told
6. explained
8. started
9. tell
10. knew

Page 45
I. Words students select will vary.
II. Check students' illustrations.

Page 48
1. Devin and Shaneka
2. Devin
3. Rude Dude
4. Shaneka, the time
5. Devin, Devin's
6. Shaneka, the poem, Shaneka's poem
7. Shaneka and Devin, Devin, the judges', opinion

Page 49
1. aunt
2. right
3. watch
4. walk
5. listen
6. Wednesday
7. February
8. often
9. answer
10. island
11. could
12. fudge

Page 52
Answers will vary. Suggested answers:
1. something worn for safety
2. something that can be defended or excused
3. being without fault
4. allowed to be included
5. the act of keeping in memory
6. something that causes harm

Page 53

	Circled	Corrected
1.	than	then
2.	here	hear
3.	yourselfs	yourselves
4.	hole	whole
5.	anybudy	anybody
6.	cafateria	cafeteria
7.	rote	wrote
8.	accept	except
9.	defence	defense
10.	necks	next

Page 56
Answers will vary. Suggested answers:
1.
   a. goes down
   b. goes up
   c. you
2.
   a. goes down
   b. goes up
   c. 3

Page 57
1. voice
2. alien
3. language
4. Theoretically
5. sublime
6. creature
7. slice
8. stomps
★ word: clueless

Page 60
Answers will vary.

Page 61
1. scarlet: intense red
2. azure: light or sky blue
3. chartreuse: yellow-green
4. khaki: tan or light brown
5. indigo: deep blue-violet
6. magenta: reddish purple
7. russet: reddish brown
8. turquoise: blue-green
9. taupe: brownish gray
10. fuchsia: deep purplish pink

Page 64
The exact wording of students' summaries will vary; however, they should be similar to the one below.

Beginning: The author is happy with his Human Remote Control.

Middle: The author mutes his yelling teacher.

End: The author is going to try to mute his dad.

Page 65
Categories may vary slightly. Suggested answers:
1. feelings of gladness
2. ways to talk
3. body parts/face parts
4. ways to move
5. shelters
6. family members
7. feelings
8. jobs/occupations
9. ways to show force
10. words that show strength of character

Page 68

Students' wording may vary slightly. Suggested wording is provided below.

1. Alvin says a nerd is a highly intelligent person who is very scholarly and does well in many domains. A geek is a person who obsesses in one area.
2. Alvin is described as a big kid who is very coordinated.
3. Alvin gives a Vulcan salute, something that geeks do and not nerds.
4. Alvin's dream is to win the Nobel Prize for Physics.
5. Alvin likes science and thinks about it in everything, such as seeing potential energy in a stretched rubber band.
6. Alvin thinks it would be boring to be normal.
7. Alvin gave himself the name "Nerd-One."

Page 69

1. coordinated
2. scholarly
3. obsesses
4. reluctant
5. ironic
6. potential
7. physics
8. unbelievably

Page 72

1. and
2. Now
3. which
4. Then
5. but
6. However
7. which
8. However
9. After

Page 73

1. wet
2. changing
3. cooling
4. tiny
5. theory; not related to heat
6. dry lake bed
7. liquid

Page 76

Double negatives replaced with:

1. don't ever or never
2. wasn't ever or was never
3. doesn't ever or never
4. can't ever or can never
5. isn't ever or is never

Page 77

Mathematics Words: percent, equation, symmetry, integer, numeral, square, fraction, angle, decimal

Geography Words: compass, climate, landform, island, arctic, globe, equator, glacier, erosion

Astronomy Words: lunar, asteroid, satellite, orbit, comet, solar, eclipse, meteor, telescope

Notes: Students may include compass in Geography or Mathematics Words.

Page 80

Student responses will vary.

Page 81

1. carbon
2. fusion
3. conservation
4. fossil
5. global
6. renewable
7. recycle
8. consume
9. species

Page 84

1. beneath
2. miniature
3. seldom
4. starve
5. hinder
6. accumulate
7. respond
8. portion
9. seize
10. remark
11. hold
12. display

Page 85

Page 88

1. troposphere: This is the lowest layer of atmosphere…
2. stratosphere: This is a layer of atmosphere that runs from…
3. mesosphere: Of the five layers of atmosphere, this falls in the middle…
4. thermosphere: This atmospheric layer, which begins…
5. exosphere: Of the five layers of atmosphere, this is the outermost…

Page 89

The layers from top to bottom: exosphere, thermosphere, mesosphere, stratosphere, troposphere.

Page 92

Students should use the proofreader's symbol of three lines drawn under a letter to be capitalized for the initial letter of these proper nouns in the story:

Sam Hawkins, Dimitri Rosen, Mars, Park Mall, each occurrence of Sam, Dimitri, Beth, Julie, and Maria, Julie Marcos, Maria Beckham, Beth Hawkins, and Hawkins

Page 93

1. nagged at (2)
2. to make different (2)
3. units of measurement (1)
4. returned (3)
5. the part that is left (2)
6. maintain a position (2)
7. being in accordance with what is good (2)

Page 96

Students should use the proofreader's symbol of three lines drawn under a letter to be capitalized for the first letter of these proper nouns in the passage:

United States, Constitution, Bill of Rights, Congress, Supreme Court,

Founding Fathers, Constitution, Bill of Rights, America's, National Archives, Washington, D. C., Thomas Jefferson's, Americans, United States, July

Page 97

I.

1. bad
2. deserve
3. mean
4. no say
5. unfairly

II. Sentences will vary.

Page 100

1. infection
2. complication
3. visitation
4. reaction
5. fascination
6. revision
7. education
8. accusation
9. classification
10. discussion
11. agitation
12. comprehension

Page 101

1. annihilate—to defeat by completely destroying
2. tension—a state of anxiety usually accompanied by nervous shaking
3. detention—a form of punishment in which someone must….
4. agitation—having anxious, worrisome, or uneasy feelings
5. citation—official acknowledgement; in law, an order to appear
6. tension
7. annihilate
8. citation
9. agitation
10. detention

Page 104

I. common 2, denominator 5, fractions 2, reactions 3, simple 2, everybody 4, function 2, calculator 4

II. 2 syllables: com/mon, frac/tions, sim/ple, func/tion; 3 syllables: re/ac/tions; 4 syllables: eve/ry/bod/y, cal/cu/la/tor; 5 syllables: de/nom/in/a/tor,

Page 105

	Underlined	Corrected
1.	denomnator	denominator
2.	howl	how
3.	tim	time
4.	stranj	strange
5.	waist	waste
6.	sutch	such
7.	zilliun	zillion
8.	simpel	simple
9.	Everybudy's	Everybody's
10.	Iv'e	I've
11.	funktion	function

Page 108

Sentences will vary.

Page 109

1. city
2. city
3. country
4. city
5. country
6. state
7. state
8. city
9. country
10. city
11. country
12. country
13. city
14. state
15. city
16. state
17. city
18. country
19. city
20. country

Page 112

Answers will vary.

Page 113

1. drowning us in tests
2. parents, principals, and presidents
3. Am I talking to a wall?
4. in this moment of our youth
5. hunger for the truth
6. Ignite the flame!

Answer Key *(cont.)*

Page 116
1. it
2. Our
3. His, He
4. He
5. He
6. She
7. we
8. Our, We

Page 117
Students' responses will vary.

Page 120
Students' responses will vary.

Page 121
1 **Down**—chic

2 **Across**—reflection

3 **Down**—egomania

4 **Down**—Transylvania

5 **Across**—chatter

6 **Across**—personal

7 **Across**—fangs

8 **Across**—insensitive

Page 124
Where: in school, in the world, at my school, in the park

What: of youth, to scream, of peer pressure, of stuff, about being young

Page 125
1. worry, world, every, hear
2. where, there, worrying, universal, extracurricular, Homework, Teachers, ever-present, over-powering, peer pressure
3. park, worry, world, forget

Page 128
1. means
2. is
3. went
4. hurts
5. sprained
6. kept
7. trying
8. is
9. pack

Page 129
1. clueless
2. breathless
3. borderless
4. careless
5. tasteless
6. guiltless
7. flawless
8. harmless
9. hopeless
10. sleepless
11. cordless
12. worthless
13. senseless
14. powerless
15. hairless
16. goalless
17. odorless
18. colorless
19. homeless
20. friendless
21 endless
22. fearless

Page 132
1. terrible
2. private
3. field
4. dairy
5. flat
6. little
7. lovely
8. bright green
9. peaceful
10. private
11. perfect

Page 133
Answers will vary.

Page 136
Answers will vary.

Page 137
Answers will vary.

References Cited

Bottomley, D., and J. Osborn. 1993. *Implementing reciprocal teaching with fourth- and fifth-grade students in content area reading*. ERIC document 361668.

Bromley, K. 2004. Rethinking vocabulary instruction. *The Language and Literacy Spectrum* 14:3–12.

Carter, C. 1997. "Why reciprocal teaching?" *Educational Leadership* 54(6): 64–68.

Harris, T., and R. Hodges (Eds.). 1995. *The literacy dictionary: The vocabulary of reading and writing*. Newark, DE: International Reading Association.

Harvey, S., and A. Goudvis. 2000. *Strategies that work: Teaching comprehension to enhance understanding and engagement*. Portland, ME: Stenhouse Publishers.

Herrell, A., and M. Jordan. 2004. *Fifty strategies for teaching English language learners*. 2nd ed. Upper Saddle, NJ: Pearson Education, Inc.

Hosenfeld, C. 1993. *Activities and materials for implementing adapted versions of reciprocal teaching in beginning, intermediate, and advanced levels of instruction in English, Spanish, and French as a second/foreign language*. ERIC document ED370354.

Jensen, E. 1998. *Teaching with the brain in mind*. Alexandria, VA: Association for Supervision and Curriculum Development.

Keene, E., and S. Zimmermann. 1997. *Mosaic of thought*. Portsmouth, NH: Heinemann.

Mid-continent Research for Education and Learning (McREL). 2009. Compendium K-12 standards, content knowledge standards, language arts. Level II (Grade 3–5) and Level III (Grades 6–8) Denver, CO: McREL.

National Institute of Child Health and Human Development. 2000, Updated 2006. *Teaching children to read: An evidence-based assessment of the scientific research literature on reading and its implications for reading instruction*. Report of the National Reading Panel. Washington, D.C.: U.S. Government Print Office.

Pressley, M. 2001. Comprehension instruction: What makes sense now, what might make sense soon. *Reading Online*. 5(2): http://www.readingonline.org/articles/handbook/pressley/index.html

Rasinski, T. V. 2003. *The fluent reader*. New York, NY: Scholastic Professional Books.

Richek, M. 2005. Words are wonderful: Interactive, time-efficient strategies to teach meaning vocabulary. *The Reading Teacher* 58(5): 414–423.

Rosenshine, B., and C. Meister. 1994. Reciprocal teaching: A review of the research. *Review of Educational Research*. 64(4): 479–530.

WIDA—housed within the Wisconsin Center for Education Research. 2007. English language proficiency standards. The Board of Regents of the University of Wisconsin System, http://www.wida.us/standards/elp.aspx

Contents of the CDs

Contents of the Teacher Resource CD

Poems and Activity Pages

Lesson	Pages	Filename
1	19–21	lesson1.pdf
2	23–25	lesson2.pdf
3	27–29	lesson3.pdf
4	31–33	lesson4.pdf
5	35–37	lesson5.pdf
6	39–41	lesson6.pdf
7	43–45	lesson7.pdf
8	47–49	lesson8.pdf
9	51–53	lesson9.pdf
10	55–57	lesson10.pdf
11	59–61	lesson11.pdf
12	63–65	lesson12.pdf
13	67–69	lesson13.pdf
14	71–73	lesson14.pdf
15	75–77	lesson15.pdf
16	79–81	lesson16.pdf
17	83–85	lesson17.pdf
18	87–89	lesson18.pdf
19	91–93	lesson19.pdf
20	95–97	lesson20.pdf
21	99–101	lesson21.pdf
22	103–105	lesson22.pdf
23	107–109	lesson23.pdf
24	111–113	lesson24.pdf
25	115–117	lesson25.pdf
26	119–121	lesson26.pdf
27	123–125	lesson27.pdf
28	127–129	lesson28.pdf
29	131–133	lesson29.pdf
30	135–137	lesson30.pdf

Additional Resources

Item	Filename
Page-turning Book	tweenmachine.html
Instructional Plan	instructional.pdf
McREL Chart	mcrelchart.pdf
Activity Skill Corr. Chart	activitychart.pdf

Contents of the Audio CD

Track	Title
01	Introduction
02	Shaneka "The Mouth" Byrd
03	Big! Mean! Tween! Machine!
04	Denied
05	Hurricane Henrietta
06	Big Sister
07	Devin "I'm OK-You're-OK" Shay
08	Rude Dude
09	Sisters and Brothers
10	Girl Monsters from Outer Space
11	Between the Lines
12	Remote Control
13	Alvin "Nerd-One" Lofton
14	Crystal Cool
15	Knowing the Why
16	Brain Power
17	Protein Passion
18	Stairway to the Stars
19	Armando "El Fuego" Martí
20	Teacher Police
21	Snakehair Lady
22	Find the Common Denominator
23	Questions and Answers
24	The Flame
25	Veronica "Queen of the Dead" Page
26	Vampire Friends
27	The Joy of Youth
28	Sprained Heart
29	Private Poison
30	Where Eagles Fly